Dinosaurs in the Morning

Also by Whitney Balliett

The Sound of Surprise

dinosaurs
in the morning

**41
Pieces
on
Jazz**

by Whitney <u>Balliett</u>

J. B. Lippincott Company

Philadelphia and New York

For Julie and Blue and Will,
in hopes they find their own
Sidney Catletts

Contents

Note

THAT JAZZ should be written about critically is doubtful. It is an elusive, subjective form, whose delights are immediate and often fleeting. It seizes the emotions and the heart—but rarely the head—and few people need written instructions on how to feel. Moreover, jazz, unlike many musics, must be listened to and listened to before its secrets, which are many, become plain, and no amount of reading will do this for you. Nonetheless, the music is mercurial, and the curiosity about it is widespread. As a result, perhaps an attempt should be made to pin down its sights and sounds on paper. I am also pretty well convinced that some sort of running commentary on the music's ceaseless change has value; after all, jazz is the liveliest and possibly most influential music in the world, and tomorrow it may be gone. To be sure, no such commentary can be wholly accurate or wholly agreeable. Critics are biased, and so are readers. (Indeed, a critic is a bundle of biases held loosely together by a sense of taste.) But intelligent readers soon discover how to allow for the windage of their own and a critic's prejudices.

There is no point in a survey here of what is happening in jazz. That, hopefully, is what this book is. But perhaps I should say that the music is in an extraordinary ferment that is centered on the semi-atonal abstract jazz of Ornette Coleman,

11

Cecil Taylor, George Russell, Charlie Mingus, and Don Ellis, among an increasing number of others. These men are busy taking the music apart and putting it back together differently, and their realignments will dictate the jazz of the future. (Third-stream music—Gunther Schuller's prodigy—is roughly parallel to this movement. It is and is not a part of it.) Concurrently, the earliest forms of the music—New Orleans jazz, Dixieland, boogie-woogie, Kansas City jazz, the country blues—are sadly dead or dying. Certain swing musicians thrive and even grow, while those occasional groups, like the Modern Jazz Quartet, continue to appear as epitomizers of the best that has come before. It is silly to argue that art progresses—Degas is no better than De la Tour, just different—and jazz is no exception. The beauties of Louis Armstrong and Red Allen in 1933, the Basie band of 1938, the Ellington band of 1940–1942, Charlie Parker, Dizzy Gillespie, and Sidney Catlett in 1945, and Mingus, Coleman, and John Lewis now are equal and quite dissimilar. Listeners blind to this don't know what they are missing.

These pieces are a selection from my jazz criticism and reporting published in *The New Yorker* from 1957 to 1962 (one piece is from 1957 and one from 1958). They have all been revised, some from stem to stern, and they are not in strict chronological order. None of them has been reprinted before.

Naturally, this book exists because of the musicians who are and are not mentioned in it. I am also beholden to Martin Williams, who *thinks* about jazz more than any other public observer. And I am more than grateful to Rogers Whitaker and William Shawn, of *The New Yorker*.

W. B.

Part One: 1957-1959

in the kind of world that Jack Kerouac *imagines* he has lived in." His eyes shot up, and he sprayed a dozen rounds of laughter about the room. "A good many people, including the musicians I work with, think of jazz poetry at first as something only a weedhead would do. Not long ago, I worked with a symphony bassist, and he told me afterward, 'You know, I was really scared, but it's been one of the greatest musical experiences of my life.' I didn't start this thing. Renegade monks were doing it in the Middle Ages. Charles Cros, a nineteenth-century poet, read his stuff (things like '*Le Hareng Saur*': 'There was a great white wall, bare, bare, bare' —ha-ha-ha-ha-ha-ha) to *bal-musette* bands. There have been countless talking-blues singers in the South. Maxwell Bodenheim did it in the twenties and Langston Hughes in the thirties, and even I did it in the twenties, at the Green Mask, in Chicago, with Frank Melrose, a K.C. pianist. I've been reading poetry to jazz for two years now, starting in The Cellar, in San Francisco, with a quintet. Since then, I've done all of the West Coast, St. Louis, Chicago, Minneapolis. The most important instrument in my accompaniment is the bass. The bass goes right up your leg and sends out the voice. Modern jazz has outgrown everything. The audience can't get into the music without verbal contact. The poetry gives you that, and the jazz gets the poetry out of those seminars taught by aging poets for budding poets in cornbelt colleges. I plan a good deal of the musical accompaniment, which isn't all jazz by any means. I use bits of Satie, Webern, Boccherini. Each musician has a copy of what I'm reciting, with cues and musical notations on it. I read Ruthven Todd, Larry Durrell, Ferlinghetti, and some of my own stuff, including a lot of translations. A friend warned me about New York. 'You've got to be careful, man,' he said. 'They've been having meetings to keep Rexroth out.' Ha-ha-ha-ha-ha-ha-ha!"

Rexroth asked me to stop in at the Five Spot before his first show that night, and I was met there, at about nine-thirty, by Ivan Black, a stocky, black-mustached representative of the Five Spot, who ushered me to a table near the bandstand, a raised platform roughly the size of a large window seat. "I've got to go and wake Rexroth up," he told us. "He's sleeping at a friend's, over on Second Avenue. I'll be right back." "The Five Spot is long and narrow, with a bar, sheltered by a fringed canopy, running down most of one wall; three gold-colored macelike objects suspended from a maroon ceiling; and the rest of the wall space spattered with posters and programs of various sorts. "He wasn't asleep at all," Black's voice said after a while, in a relieved way, and Rexroth, wearing impenetrable dark glasses, sat down beside me. "These shades protect you in a club," he said. "I've decided they relax you. I read my stuff. You can't do it out of your head. You get swinging, and you don't know what you're talking about."

Rexroth then said it was time to begin. Black excused himself and, while squeezing onto the platform to introduce Rexroth, accidentally brushed a thick sheaf of manuscripts off a wobbly music stand.

"Damn it, Ivan! What are you doing?" Rexroth bellowed as Black backed and filled on the manuscripts.

The manuscripts were replaced, a drum roll crashed out, and Black introduced Rexroth as a horse wrangler and the Daddy-O of the jazz-poetry movement.

Daddy-O

Rexroth got up on the platform, plunged his left hand into his left coat pocket, took as wide a stance as space permitted, stuck his stomach out, and read, in a strong singsong voice, a Ruthven Todd poem; Carl Sandburg's "Mag," accompanied by an Ellington blues; a poem by Pablo Neruda; a poem of his own; and a twelfth-century Chinese poem, accompanied only by the bass, which played long passages between such lines as "But why do the birds all hate me?," "Why do the flowers betray me?," "Why do the peach and cherry blossoms prostrate me?"

The Great Gillespie

OF ALL the uncommunicative, secret-society terms that jazz has surrounded itself with, few are more misleading than "bebop." Originally a casual onomatopoeic word used to describe the continually shifting rhythmic accents in the early work of Charlie Parker, Dizzy Gillespie, Kenny Clarke, and Thelonious Monk, it soon became a generic term, whose tight, rude sound implied something harsh and unattractive. (Jazz scholars, who are nonpareil at unearthing irrelevancies, have discovered that the two syllables first appeared in jazz as a bit of mumbo-jumbo in a vocal recorded in the late twenties.) Although many admirers of Parker and Gillespie—and occasionally Parker and Gillespie themselves—helped this misapprehension along in the mid-forties through their playing, bebop was, in the main, a graceful rococo explosion. It replaced the old Republican phrasing with long, teeming melodic lines, melted the four-four beat into more fluid rhythms, and added fresh harmonies, the combination producing an arabesque music that had a wild beauty suggested in jazz up to that time only by certain boogie-woogie pianists (another of jazz's better-known code terms) and by such soloists, often considered freakish, as Pee Wee Russell, Dickie Wells, Jabbo Smith, and Roy Eldridge. Bebop was an upheaval in jazz that matched the arrival of Louis Armstrong, Duke Ellington, Coleman Hawkins, and Lester Young, but it was not, as it is frequently taken to be, a total musical revolution. (The most usable elements of the movement have long since been absorbed into jazz, and the term itself has fallen into disuse, but a variation, known as "hard bop," persists.) To be sure, it introduced radical techniques, but it stuck close to the blues, which it dressed up in flatted chords and various rhythmic furbelows. The chord structures of popular standards, which provided the rest of its diet, were slightly altered, and were given new titles and often barefacedly copyrighted by their "composers." This renovating process, begun in the mid-thirties by men like Duke Ellington and Count Basie, proliferated in the bebop era. Thus, "Indiana" reappeared as "Donna Lee" and "Ice Freezes Red"; "How High the Moon" became "Bean at the Met," "Ornithology," and "Bird Lore"; and "Just You, Just Me" turned into "Evidence," "Spotlite," and "Mad Bebop." The music made little attempt at fresh ensemble voicings, but relied instead on complex unison figures—in the manner of the John Kirby band—that sounded like fattened-up extensions of the solos they enclosed. On top of that, bebop musicians continued to investigate, though in a sometimes obtuse, hyper-

The Great Gillespie   19

thyroid way, the same lyricism pursued by their great predecessors. A final confusing peculiarity of bebop is that although Parker, Gillespie, and Monk, each of whom possessed enormous talent, emerged at about the same time, they never enjoyed the spotlight simultaneously, as did such slightly older men as Hawkins, Eldridge, Art Tatum, and Sidney Catlett. Gillespie had become celebrated by the late forties; Parker was at the height of his fame when he died, in 1955; and it is only recently that Monk has slid wholly into view. Meanwhile, Gillespie, who remains one of the handful of supreme jazz soloists, seems—possibly because of the widespread emulation of an uneven ex-student of his, Miles Davis—to have been put to pasture.

When Gillespie appeared on the first bebop recordings, in 1944, he gave the impression—largely because a long recording ban had just ended—of springing up full-blown. He had, however, been slowly developing his style for some seven or eight years. Although Gillespie was for a time an unashamed copy of Eldridge, the records he made in the late thirties with Cab Calloway—in which he tossed off strange, wrong-sounding notes and bony phrases that seemed to begin and end in arbitrary places—prove that his own bent, mixed perhaps with dashes of Lester Young and Charlie Christian, was already in view. By 1944, the transformation was complete, and Gillespie had entered his second phase.

Few trumpeters have been blessed with so much technique. Gillespie never merely started a solo— he erupted into it. A good many bebop solos began with four- or eight-bar breaks, and Gillespie, taking full advantage of this approach (a somewhat similar technique had been used, to great effect, in much

New Orleans jazz, but had largely fallen into disuse), would hurl himself into the break, after a split-second pause, with a couple of hundred notes that corkscrewed through several octaves, sometimes in triple time, and that were carried, usually in one breath, past the end of the break and well into the solo itself. The result, in such early Gillespie efforts as "One-Bass Hit" and "Night in Tunisia," were complex, exuberant, and well-designed. (Several of Gillespie's flights were transcribed note for note into ensemble passages for various contemporary big bands, an honor previously granted to the likes of Bix Beiderbecke.) Gillespie's style at the time gave the impression—with its sharp, slightly acid tone, its cleavered phrase endings, its efflorescence of notes, and its brandishings about in the upper register—of being constantly on the verge of flying apart. However, his playing was held together by his extraordinary rhythmic sense, which he shared with the other founders of bebop. When one pinned down the melodic lines of his solos, they revealed a flow of notes that was not so much a melody, in the conventional sense, as a series of glancing but articulate sounds arranged in sensible rhythmic blocks that alternated from on-the-beat playing to offbeat punctuation, from double-and-triple-time to half time. One felt that Gillespie first spelled out his rhythmic patterns in his head and then filled in their spaces with appropriate notes. A hard, brilliant, flag-waving style, in which emotion was frequently hidden in floridity, it persisted until four or five years ago, when Gillespie popped, again seemingly full-blown, into his third, and present, period.

A mild-mannered, roundish man, who wears thick-rimmed spectacles and a small goatee, and has a new-moon smile and a muffled, potatoey way of speaking, Gillespie is apt, when playing, to puff out his cheeks and neck into an enormous balloon, as if he were preparing himself for an ascent into the ionosphere. He has a habit, while his associates play, of performing jigs or slow, swaying shufflings, accented by occasional shouts of encouragement—bits of foolishness that he discards, like a mask, when he takes up his own horn, an odd-shaped instrument whose specially designed bell points in the direction of the upper bleachers. Gillespie, at forty-two, an age at which a good many jazz musicians begin falling back on a card file of phrases—their own and others'—built up through the years, is playing with more subtlety and invention than at any time in his past. He has learned one of the oldest and best tricks in art—how to give the effect of great power by *implying* generous amounts of untapped energy. This method is opposed to the dump-everything approach, which swamps, rather than whets, the listener's appetite. His tone has taken on a middle-age spread; his baroque flow of notes has been judiciously edited; his phrase endings seem less abrupt; and he now cunningly employs a sense of dynamics that mixes blasts with whispers, upper-register shrieks with plaintive asides. However, his intensity, together with his rhythmic governor, which still sets the basic course of his solos, remains unchanged. Provided a solo does not open with a break, which he will attack with the same old ferocity, Gillespie may now begin with a simple phrase, executed in an unobtrusive double time and repeated in rifflike fashion. Then he will lean back into half time and deliver a bellowing upper-register figure, which may be topped with a triple-time descending arpeggio composed of innumerable notes that dodge and dodge and then lunge ahead again. These continue without pause for several measures, terminating in a series of sidling half-valved notes, which have a bland complacency, like successful businessmen exchanging compliments. In the next chorus, he may reverse the procedure by opening with a couple of shouts, and then subside into a blinding run, seemingly made up of hundred-and-twenty-eighth notes, that will end in high scalar exercises. And so it goes. Gillespie rarely repeats himself in the course of a solo. In fact, he is able to construct half a dozen or more choruses in which the element of surprise never falters.

Gillespie is in good form on three fairly recent records—"Crosscurrents" (American Recording Society), "Sonny Side Up," and "Have Trumpet Will Excite!" (Verve). Of the three, "Crosscurrents," is the most satisfactory. On hand with Gillespie, for two originals, a blues, and four standards (three of them done as a short medley of solos), are Sonny Stitt, John Lewis, Percy Heath, the guitarist Skeeter Best, and the drummer Charlie Persip. In long solos in "Tour de Force" (medium tempo) and "Dizzy Meets Sonny" (very fast), Gillespie gives his all—particularly in the latter, where he ranges from sotto-voce figures, at the start of the first chorus, to upper-register harum-scarum in the third, bumblebee fluctuations in the fourth, and staggering runs, which dissolve into a thumb-twiddling phrase, in the fifth. In "How Deep Is the Ocean," Gillespie takes just one chorus, at a slow tempo, and, winding closely around the melody, plays with a gentle poignancy, achieved by moving precisely back and forth between loud phrases and furtive ones. The record closes with a slow blues, "Blues for Bird," in which Gillespie constructs three choruses proving that one needn't, in the manner of many of his students, add curlicues to the blues to make them effective. (Almost all of Gillespie's admirers fall short of him in another way, too; they are unable to sustain a persuasive melodic line on slow ballads, and, as a result, often resemble a Salvation Army band on a cold day.)

Although much of "Sonny Side Up" is given over to Stitt (on tenor saxophone here) and Sonny Rollins, Gillespie comes through with three consummate choruses in "After Hours," the Avery Parrish-Erskine Hawkins blues. Using a mute, Gillespie darts from a level first chorus to a red-faced high note, opening the second chorus, that falls away to sly, disconnected notes, each one on the beat, and into a final chorus, where, stretching out, he strikingly recalls, probably on purpose, Roy Eldridge. He plays almost as well in the three remaining numbers (two standards and an original), and in "Sunny Side of the Street" he sings the vocal, delivering the first sixteen bars in a nasal monotone that seems, in its perversity, more melodic than the tune's real melody.

For some reason, Gillespie loafs through much of his own record, "Have Trumpet, Will Excite!" He is accompanied by an adequate rhythm section, whose guitarist, Les Spann, occasionally doubles on flute. All eight numbers are standards, the best of which are a wry "My Heart Belongs to Daddy" (much of Gillespie's work has a forthright mocking quality), a brisk "St. Louis Blues," and a slow, almost back-scratching "There Is No Greater Love." There isn't an unforgettable moment on the record, but there aren't many passages that could be surpassed by Gillespie's contemporaries, most of whom would be in other lines of work if it weren't for him.

A Celebration for Monk

FOR ALMOST TWO DECADES, Thelonious Monk has been carefully constructing a witty, indivisible, and totally original world. As a performer, and an eccentric one, Monk is misleading. Most eccentrics embroider the unreal for the sake of itself, but his waywardness is the natural outcome of forcing traditional materials like the blues to their farthest logical limits. Stripped of their dissonant harmonies and displaced rhythms, Monk's works are basically straightforward, often charming melodies, which, in the process of composition, he stretches, compresses, and twists, so that by the time they are on paper they have become industrious improvisations of what first entered his head. But that is only the halfway mark. When Monk plays one of his pieces, he takes a single aspect of it and goes to work on it again to see how much more pressure it can bear and still retain its fundamental qualities.

Unfortunately, "An Evening with Thelonious Monk," a concert held last Saturday at Town Hall and devoted entirely to Monk's compositions, played by a quartet and a ten-piece group, only hinted at this height. Like many similar celebrations—and this was the first that Monk has ever been treated to—the evening never seemed to disentangle itself from Significance; one kept waiting for the speeches to blow away, as it were, and the fun to begin. The trouble was not with Monk, a remarkably consistent pianist, who is always close to his best, but with his accompanists, whom he was forced to tow throughout the concert. Five of the eleven compositions played were performed by Monk, Charlie Rouse, Sam Jones (bass), and Arthur Taylor (drums), who were joined in the remaining numbers by Donald Byrd (trumpet); Phil Woods (alto saxophone); Pepper Adams (baritone saxophone); Eddie Bert (trombone); a French horn; and a tuba. The quartet, which offered such selections as "In Walked Bud," "Blue Monk," " 'Round Midnight," and "Straight, No Chaser," was hampered by two things—Rouse and Taylor. Rouse is an unobtrusive and often dull compound of the conventional aspects of Lester Young, Charlie Parker, and Sonny Rollins. He produced some good phrases in "In Walked Bud" and "Blue Monk," but the rest of the time he muttered along anxiously, forcing one's attention to Monk's accompaniment, which was exhilarating. (There is a distinct I-dare-you quality to Monk, as a player and composer, that either swamps a fellow-musician or causes him to grow to a new size.) Taylor, on the other hand, is a monotonous fusion of the styles of Art Blakey and Max Roach. He depends on (1) the ride cymbal, (2) the relentless use of bass-drum explosions, or "bombs," and (3) ratcheting accents on the snare drum, all of which, instead of supporting the soloists, became an independent river of noise. (Monk himself is a one-man rhythm factory, and possibly the only drummer who knows how to work with him is Blakey, who provides a *simpático* background, which, now and then, he breaks with fast double-time or off-rhythm excursions on the snare or snare rim, in the fashion of an alert boxer who sees an opening and lands one.)

These shortcomings were doubled when the large group came onstage for such numbers as "Friday the 13th," "Little Rootie Tootie," and "Crepuscule with Nellie." The arrangements were a collaboration between Monk and Hall Overton, a classical composer and pianist who dabbles frequently in jazz, and although they had the virtue of furnishing showcases for Monk's compositions, they were, with one exception, pale small-band scorings—unison passages sprinkled with mild counterpoint—in which almost no effort was made to strengthen the various competent but second-rate soloists. The exception occurred in the last couple of choruses of "Little Rootie Tootie," when the whole group executed an admirable transcription of Monk's solo part in his first recording of the tune. The number revelled in Monk. In the opening chorus, the ensemble played an unadorned version of the melody; then Monk presented a spontaneous distillation of it; and, finally, the whole group magnified his earlier effort into a jarring, dissonant contrapuntal form that sounded like a dozen Monks playing at once and that explained what the rest of the evening had failed to do. Before the last number, an encore of the same tune, Monk strolled out from the wings and, speaking for the first time, said "Thank you" into a microphone at center stage, and then, his back to the audience, leaned toward another microphone inside the piano, and offhandedly repeated his thanks. Monk had survived.

Bittersweet

WHEN ATONALITY, an against-the-grain system, whose appeal lies in its perversity, and jazz improvisation, which also depends upon the perverse, are mixed together, the results can be as repellent but irresistible as sucking a lemon. One of those musicians is Cecil Taylor, who appeared with a quintet last Friday at the Circle in the Square. A flat-topped, bespectacled man, Taylor is an intense performer who, in his fervent moments, emits a singsong hum, wags his head slowly back and forth, and draws in his cheeks and opens his mouth, as if it held a hot potato, while his hands, instead of merely rising, recoil from the keyboard as if it, too, were hot. Taylor's style at first seems a discordant welter of Stravinsky, Debussy, and Bartók, lightened with occasional out-and-out jazz phrases. It soon becomes clear, though, that he is bending these approaches toward a heretofore unknown type of jazz improvisation. Going several steps beyond Thelonious Monk, who has also influenced him, he attempts to string together varied islands of sound that stretch from cathedral-like chords—often rat-tat-tatted through three or four octaves by both hands, working in unison and separately—to glass-tapping single-note figures that resemble Debussy, but with the blur focussed out. Taylor, in the fashion of Art Tatum's arhythmic escapades, does not play with a direct beat. Instead, he gradually converts his irregularities—leaps between chords, single notes, and registers; sudden silences; a subtle use of crescendo and diminuendo—into an over-all rhythmic design, which, like a jigsaw puzzle's, emerges only when a solo is completed. And, again in common with Tatum, whose inability to subordinate himself to the collective demands of a group frequently recalled a fat man fighting his way into tight clothes, Taylor is primarily a solo performer.

The most successful parts of the evening were three unaccompanied piano numbers and Taylor's solos on the eight selections done by the group. (All of the tunes, which varied from blues to refashionings of standards like "You and the Night and the Music," were written or arranged by Taylor.) The rest of the time, his associates, who included Ted Curson (trumpet), Bill Barron (tenor saxophone), Ahmed Abdul-Malik (bass), and Rudy Collins (drums), struggled with solos based on atonal bases and with contrapuntal ensembles that moved between the hair-pulling exercises of Charlie Mingus and the clasping and unclasping two-horn work favored in the mid-forties by Lennie Tristano. Curson, a liquid, uneven musician, perched between Dizzy Gillespie and Miles Davis, was creditable, particularly on the three blues played, while Barron, who has some of the faraway characteristics of Stan Getz, tended to sound more and more remote. Abdul-Malik, however, went at Taylor's melodic lines with such dedication that he produced a rough, slapping, wooden sound that often upstaged Taylor. But it was Taylor's evening. Again and again, he shook one with his unpredictability. During one of the unaccompanied numbers, which, though unidentified, sounded something like "All or Nothing at All," he developed in his right hand a series of sour, staccato chords, while in the left hand he stabbed out, with a daggerlike finger, a slow, dissonant single-note figure that set up an irregular seesaw rhythm that made one feel as if giants were walking the earth again.

Toshiko

NONE of the foreign jazz musicians who occasionally pelt our shores has been more comely, modest, or accomplished than Toshiko Akiyoshi, a twenty-seven-year-old Japanese pianist. Much of the time since her arrival, Toshiko, as she is known, has been in Boston, where, by day, she has been studying musical composition and theory at the Berklee School of Music and, by night, filling a night club named Storyville. Last week, pried loose from the North, Toshiko opened at the Hickory House with her trio, a handful of appropriate kimonos, and a gorgeous scarlet, gold, and white ceremonial *obi* (a broad, heavy silk sash worn about the middle). I went to see her at the Park Sheraton on the afternoon of her début, and she was a vision in black: neat black dress, black patent-leather shoes, wide black eyes, and glistening black hair that fell in a dancing ponytail to her waist. Stocky and quick-moving, Toshiko gave a shy, brilliant smile and lit on the edge of a chair with the air of someone about to be served tea. I asked her how she had become a jazz pianist. "Oh, was by accident," she said, in warm, telegraphic English. "In '46, I decide to go to medical school. My father very much want me to become doctor. Before school begin, I visit cousin in Beppu. She hear of Japanese dance band there that need piano player. I take piano lessons since seven years old and my cousin say, 'Do you play jazz?' I say, 'I never hear of jazz.' At audition, I play a German tango called 'Blue Sky.' The leader, Mr. Yamada, say, 'Oh, she can play piano.' So I join the band. One week later, my father find out. He was very mad. Seventeen-year-old daughter playing piano in a dance palace. Toof! But I told my mother, who is very, very understandable person, that I will quit when school starts. But I didn't. A big fourteen-piece Japanese orchestra want me, then later an Argentine tango band, then another Japanese band. In '49, I went to Tokyo and joined Mr. Ikoma and his orchestra. All this time, I play no solos, just umpcha-umpcha behind band. Then, one time, I wrote out all the notes in solo on Teddy Wilson record of 'Sweet Lorraine' and put his notes beside straight melody to compare. I study difference hard and then write down new figures of my own, learn them by heart, and play them in solo next day with band. Great success."

For the next few years, Toshiko worked in Tokyo with such indigenous groups as the Blue Coast Orchestra, the Gay Stars Orchestra, the Tokyo Jive Combo, and the Six Lemons. After that, equipped with a style akin to that of Bud Powell, she formed her own group, the Coy Quartet. "One night," she said, "Oscar Peterson, in Tokyo with Norman Granz and the Jazz at the Philharmonic group, heard me play. Of course, he was idol, and when he came to speak to me, I was shaking all over. He introduce me to Mr. Granz, and Mr. Granz say, 'Would you like to make record?' He gave me Oscar Peterson rhythm section, and two weeks later I make my first record." Three years later, after the proper amount of complicated correspondence, she was offered a four-year scholarship at the Berklee School.

Toshiko was born of Japanese parents in Dairen, a seaport in Manchuria, the youngest of four girls.

The family lived in Dairen until 1946, when they were exiled to Japan by the Chinese Nationalists. From 1945 on, Dairen was occupied by the Russians, the Red Chinese, and the Chinese Nationalists. "When Russians come, my father make my sisters and I cut off all our hair to look like boys. All day long, Russian soldiers come into our house and take things. They sell them in the park in front of our house to Manchurian merchants. My sisters and I get up about four-five o'clock every morning to make many rice balls, and hide all day up on veranda and eat them. When Red Chinese come, a Communist officer and his wife—how do you say?—requisition upstairs in our house. Then the Nationalist Chinese come, and a general move in upstairs. He was very funny man. Every night, he bring young officers home to play games like chess with me and my sisters. He say to my father many times, 'Don't sell anything in your house, please. If you need money, I will give you all you want.' He want everything in house for himself after we leave. We could take only what we could carry and three dollars apiece. The general came to the station, and gave us a case of soda, like ginger ale, for going-away present.

What are Toshiko's plans for the future? "If possible, if I good enough," she said, "I would like to finish four years at Berklee early, and play a year for experience. Maybe go to Europe, too. Then I will go home and teach young Japanese jazz musicians. There are two, three with very good potential. I have learned many things from musicians here, but I will finish my life in Japan. Here is too fast. I am more or less enjoying type, slow-motion type. In Tokyo are many tiny coffeehouses, hold eight, ten people. Each have hi-fi sets and enormous collection of American jazz records. You buy one cup coffee only and sit four, five hours listening to records. Is nothing like that here."

The President

"THE JAZZ GIANTS '56" (Norgran) and "Pres and Teddy: The Lester Young-Teddy Wilson Quartet" (Verve) are among the last records Lester Young made before his death, in March, 1959, at the age of forty-nine. They are, by and large, reminders that toward the end of his life Young had slipped into the melancholy position of no longer being able to outstrip his multitude of imitators. But, in a way, this doesn't matter, for none of Young's admirers, among them such men as Stan Getz, Paul Quinichette, Zoot Sims, Jimmy Giuffre, and Lee Konitz, have ever mastered the basic quality of his style—a perfect balance between tension and relaxation. Instead, they have either emphasized the heated side of his playing, sometimes to the point of caricature (Quinichette), or thinned out his seemingly bland aspects (Getz, Giuffre, Konitz) into a colorless drawl. (These last three students of Young led tenor and alto saxophonists like Bob Cooper, Bud Shank, Lennie Niehaus, and Jack Montrose to become the chassis for the cool West Coast school, which refined itself out of existence a year or two ago.) Accordingly, Young's imitators, who ironically began appearing in the mid-forties, when Young was beginning to falter, have done a good deal of unintentional harm by producing countless inferior images of his work, which have distorted the uncanny abilities he had at the height of his career.

Young, a stooped, soft-spoken, sleepy-looking man with a static, caved-in face, who affected porkpie hats and sombre, droopy coats, which gave him a monkish appearance, was his own best obfuscation. He frequently spoke a language that referred to his employers as Pres and to his associates as Lady, and that used such expressions as "Have another helping," which meant, when addressed to a soloist, "Take another chorus." And in Count Basie's band, he developed the distracting habit of veering his instrument to one side at a forty-five-degree angle, as if he were about to paddle a canoe. These irregularities were carried directly into his playing, which was unfailingly oblique. This stemmed in part from his tone. It had a dry, sandy sound, which fell between an alto and a tenor saxophone, and which recalled his early models—Bud Freeman, who has the same sort of hoarse, whitish tone, and Frankie Trumbauer. (On the clarinet, which, unfortunately, Young played infrequently, his tone—a limber, slightly metallic one that resembled Pee Wee Russell's with the kinks straightened out—was inimitably suited to the instrument.) Added to this was the singular way he attacked his notes. He gave the impression of almost trying to avoid them, even when playing directly on the beat, by slurring them, sliding just below or over them, or by pressing them together into unhurried, nearly motionless patterns. Indeed, Young's solos often resembled a collection of evasive, melodic hums that had the quality of a soundproofed room. But underneath this outwardly lazy, one-side-of-the-mouth approach, which most of his imitators mistakenly seized upon as the basis of his style, was an absolute mastery of broken-field rhythm and phrasing—the ability to emphasize the beat simply by eluding it—that is the secret of hot playing.

This apparent coolness has resulted in the axiom that Young and Coleman Hawkins are the totally divergent leaders of the cool and hot methods of playing their instrument. But both men have been, despite their surface differences, always after the identical thing—a controlled lyricism. Hawkins, with his vibrato and dark, rubicund tone, has pursued this lyricism by taking apart the chords of a tune, eliminating certain notes, adding others, and rearranging the residue into elaborate patterns pinned directly to the beat. Young, on the other hand, poked at the melody itself, in an easy, one-finger manner, until he had reshaped it into a starker design that appeared, in spite of its rhythmic liberties, to skid along parallel to the beat, as a revised and improved shadow of the original tune. Young, in fact, was among the first to demonstrate that the short, logical, on-the-beat phrases that for most of the thirties were tightly locked to the thirty-two-bar chorus could be broken into independent, juxtaposed patterns of various rhythms and lengths. A master of economy, he never fell into the excesses of the bop school, which derived in part from him and which, after a time, engaged in a battle of rhetoric by seeing how many irrelevant notes could be uttered in the space of a chorus.

In the first chorus of a slow number, Young would seem to state the melody in a straightforward way until one discovered that he was almost imperceptibly altering it by bending certain notes down, replacing others with silence, or holding on to still others for a beat or two longer than indicated. Then, the melody softened up, he would, without raising his volume or increasing his intensity, ease into superbly mixed, gradually more complex phrases occasionally fashioned out of short riffs—repeated several times with slight variations and neatly adorned by a brief vibrato—or out of long, almost level many-noted statements. These last might begin with an exuberant legato phrase, which was abruptly gathered into up-or-downstairs leaps as daring as some of the passages of Charlie Parker but that never called attention to themselves because of the peculiar flattening effect of his tone and attack. Young's intensity showed through more clearly at faster tempos. (It also broke out unforgettably in the slow blues, which he converted into swollen legato structures that rose and fell like slow, heavy breathing.) His vibrato dried up and his legato phrases were either halved or prolonged in half-time rhythms, as if he were pouring oil on the beat in an effort to still it. In fact, all of his understated, contrasted phrases—smooth, populated runs, bass honks, single notes spattered around the beat, slow-spinning sounds that lasted for perhaps a measure and a half—were forced backhandedly toward intensifying the rhythm. Some of Young's most enduring solos occurred on such Basie records as "Taxi War Dance," "Doggin' Around," and "Clap Hands, Here Comes Charlie." No matter how often they are heard, they remain classic improvisations; not a note, tone, or accent could be changed without destroying them.

Unfortunately, the reverse is often true of the aforementioned L.P.s. Joining Young on "The Jazz Giants '56" for the five selections—a blues and four standards—are Roy Eldridge, Vic Dickenson, Teddy Wilson, Freddie Greene, Gene Ramey, and Jo Jones. Young's style here first appeared in the mid-forties, and is a less wieldy version of his earlier work. It recalls Herschel Evans, who, when he died, in 1939, was Young's sparring mate in the Basie band. Young's tone is thicker and even husky, and the vibrato is more pronounced, he uses fewer notes, and his variations sometimes have a blunt air. He goes tantalizingly to work, though, on a slow rendition of "I Didn't Know What Time It Was." Just before the close of the first sixteen bars, he evokes his old unpredictability and inserts a fast, complex-phrase—seemingly executed in slow motion—and then sets off on a series of explorations during the following chorus and a half, in which, through subtle fluctuations and the repetition of simple clusters of notes, he seems to be rubbing the paint off the melody. On much of "Pres and Teddy," he reverts to the groping, slightly sour playing that characterized most of his final work, but, regardless of how diminished Young sounds, the shape and manner are unmistakable a mile away.

Bean

IMPROVISATION, the seat of jazz, is a remorseless art that demands of the performer no less than this: that, night after night, he spontaneously invent original music by balancing—with the speed of light —emotion and intelligence, form and content, and tone and attack, all of which must both charge and entertain the spirit of the listener. Improvisation comes in various shapes. There is the melodic embellishment of Louis Armstrong and Vic Dickenson; the similar but more complex thematic improvisation of Lester Young; the improvisation upon chords, as practiced by Coleman Hawkins and Charlie Parker; and the rhythmic-thematic convolutions now being put forward by Thelonious Monk and Sonny Rollins. There are, too, the collective improvisations, such as the defunct New Orleans ensemble, and its contrapuntal descendants, which are thriving in the hands of John Lewis and Charlie Mingus. Great improvisation occurs once in a blue moon; bad improvisation, which is really not improvisation at all but a rerun or imitation of old ideas, happens all the time. No art is more precarious or domineering. Indeed, there is evidence that the gifted jazz musicians who have either died or dried up early are primarily victims not of drugs and alcohol but of the insatiable furnace of improvisation. Thus, such consummate veteran improvisers as Armstrong, Dickenson, Hawkins, Buck Clayton, and Monk are, in addition to being master craftsmen, remarkable endurance runners. One of the hardiest of these is Hawkins, who, now fifty-four, continues to play with all the vitality and authority that he demonstrated during the Harding administration as a member of Mamie Smith's Jazz Hounds.

Hawkins, in fact, is a kind of super jazz musician, for he has been a bold originator, a masterly improviser, a shepherd of new movements, and a steadily developing performer. A trim, contained man, whose rare smiles have the effect of a lamp suddenly going on within, he was the first to prove that jazz could be played on the saxophone, which had been largely a purveyor of treacle. He did this with such conviction and imagination that by the early thirties he had founded one of the two great schools of saxophone playing. In 1939, Hawkins set down, as an afterthought at a recording session, a version of "Body and Soul" that achieves the impossible—perfect art. A few years later, he repeated this success with "Sweet Lorraine" and "The Man I Love." Unlike many other jazz musicians, who are apt to regard anything new with defensive animosity, Hawkins has always kept an ear to the ground for originality, and as a result he led the first official bebop recording session, which involved Dizzy Gillespie, Max Roach, and the late Clyde Hart. Soon afterward, he used the largely unknown Thelonious Monk in some important recordings. Then his playing inexplicably began to falter and he went into semi-eclipse, from which he rocketed up, without warning, in the early fifties, landing on his feet with a brand-new style (his third), whose occasional febrility suggests a man several decades younger.

Hawkins's early style was rough and aggressive. His tone tended to be harsh and bamboolike, and he used a great many staccato, slap-tongued notes. But these mannerisms eventually vanished, and by the mid-thirties he had entered his second and most famous phase. His heavy vibrato suggested the wingbeats of a big bird and his tone halls hung with dark velvet and lit by huge fires. His technique had become infallible. He never fluffed a note, his tone never shrank or overflowed—as did Chu Berry's, say—and he gave the impression that he had enough equipment to state in half a dozen different and finished ways what was in his head. This proved to be remarkable, particularly in his handling of slow ballads.

Hawkins would often begin such a number by playing one chorus of the melody, as if he were testing it. He would stuff its fabric with tone to see how much it would take, eliminate certain notes, sustain others, slur still others, and add new ones. Then, satisfied, he would shut his eyes, as if blinded by what he was about to play, and launch into improvisation with a concentration that pinned one down. (Hawkins's total lack of tentativeness—the exhilarating, blindman tentativeness of Pee Wee Russell or Roy Eldridge—suggested that he had written out and memorized his solos long before playing them.) He would construct—out of phrases crowded with single notes, glissandos, abrupt stops, and his corrugated vibrato—long, hilly figures that sometimes lasted until his breath gave out. Refilling his lungs with wind-tunnel ferocity, he would be off again—bending notes, dropping in little runs like steep, crooked staircases, adding decorative, almost calligraphic flourishes, emphasizing an occasional phrase by allowing it to escape into puffs of breath. He often closed these solos with roomy codas, into which he would squeeze fresh and frequently fancy ideas that had simply been crowded out of his earlier ruminations. If another soloist followed him, he might terminate his own statement with an abrupt ascending figure that neatly catapulted his successor. When Hawkins had finished, his solo, anchored directly and emphatically to the beat, had been worked into an elaborate version of the original melody, as though he had fitted a Victorian mansion over a modern ranch house. At fast tempos, Hawkins merely forced the same amount of music into a smaller space. There seemed to be no pause between phrases or choruses, and this produced an intensity that thickened the beat and whose vehemence was occasionally indicated by sustained growls. Yet for all this enthusiasm, Hawkins' playing during this period often left the listener vaguely dissatisfied. Perhaps it was because his style had an unceasing—and, for that time, unusual—intellectual quality, with the glint of perfection and a viselike unwillingness to let any emotion out, lest it spoil the finish on his work. One kept waiting for the passion beneath the surface to burst through, but it never did—until five years ago.

Hawkins can now be volcanic. His present style is marked primarily by a slight tightening of tone, which sometimes resembles the sound he achieved at the outset of his career; the use of certain harsh notes and phrases that, not surprisingly, suggest Charlie Parker and Sonny Rollins; and an almost dismaying display of emotion. This exuberance has been costly. In his pursuit of pure flame, Hawkins sometimes misses notes or plays them badly, and he falls back, perhaps out of fatigue, on stock phrases of his own, such as a series of abrupt, descending triplets. When everything is in mesh, however, the results are formidable.

This happens more than once in two recent Hawkins recordings—"The High and Mighty Hawk" (Felsted) and "Coleman Hawkins/Soul" (Prestige). Despite a few flat spots, the first recording, in which Hawkins is joined by Buck Clayton, Hank Jones, Ray Brown, and the drummer Mickey Sheen, is one of his superior efforts. There are a blues, three originals, and two standards. The blues, taken at a medium tempo, is a tour de force in the best sense. After the opening ensemble, Hawkins slides, with another-day, another-dollar casualness, into a soliloquy that lasts for no less than seventeen choruses, each of them totally different and each perfectly placed. The best qualities of his present work are evident—the unremittingly logical development of a three- or four-note figure (the first five

Bean 41

choruses), the near-parodying reflections of John Coltrane (tenth chorus), the tremendous bustle (eleventh and twelfth choruses), and the emotion (fifteenth and sixteenth choruses). Hawkins matches this in "You've Changed," a slow ballad, which, however, does not receive the glossy treatment he might have offered it a decade ago. Instead, for only a chorus and a half, he approaches the melody in a cautious, exploratory way, savoring its pleasant design, making minor improvements here and there, and infusing it with warmth and lyricism. Clayton and Brown play with considerable beauty. Brown's long solo in the blues number, with its darting runs, exaggerated pauses, and half-time retarding phrases, is ingenious.

The second record is aptly named. Hawkins is accompanied by Kenny Burrell, Ray Bryant, Wendell Marshall, and Osie Johnson. There are seven numbers, most of them blues. The longest is a very slow one, which is so blue—it is filled with tremolos, gospel rhythms, rock-and-roll, and screaming blue notes—that it becomes at once the epitome of all slow blues and a caricature of all slow blues. Hawkins takes a short, plaintive solo near the opening and returns later for a chorus, in which, after some moody chanting, he emits a wail that sounds like an exhalation from Hell. The shortest number on the record is totally dissimilar—a revitalization of "Green Sleeves." Hawkins simply plays embellishments on the melody, but with such pathos that one fears he will break down before it is finished. Instead, plumbing his three and a half decades of playing, Hawkins turns it into a kind of Gettysburg Address on improvisation.

Buck Clayton and Emmett Berry

GRADUATES of the Basie school (an institution that has settled, in recent years, into a ponderous bureaucracy), Buck Clayton and Emmett Berry are part of a small group of trumpet players who appeared in the wake of Louis Armstrong and who developed a singular and subtle lyricism. Some of the original group (Bobby Stark, Joe Smith, Frankie Newton) are dead, others (Doc Cheatham, Bill Coleman, Joe Thomas) are largely unknown, one (Sidney de Paris) has suffered from his recent musical associations, and another (Harold Baker) is going strong in the Ellington band. Clayton, who has made nearly a dozen successful L.P.'s under his own name in the past few years, has been the luckiest of them. A handsome man of medium height, whose face tends to float upward at the corners when he plays, giving him a Mephistophelean appearance, he performs in a style whose imperturbable continuity is based on a flawless set of balances. Unlike Coleman Hawkins or Dizzy Gillespie, he is, though a consummate musician, not a great improviser; completely aware of his own limitations (in contrast to Roy Eldridge, who sometimes sounds like a man single-handedly inflating a blimp), he restricts himself to an agile, ceaseless form of embellishment. In a medium-tempo blues, Clayton, whose tone has a smooth, hammered-gold quality, is apt to state, in a hushed, placating fashion, a short riff, which he may repeat or alter with added notes and short, skipping runs. This gives way to a lagging behind the beat, which he achieves by hitting the same note four or five times a split second after the beat. He then returns to the beat and finishes the chorus by linking related melodic figures that suggest a man humming an improvised tune to himself. In the space of several choruses, Clayton will gradually and logically work toward a climax—most jazz soloists leave off where they began—by slightly increasing his volume, incorporating high, probing notes, and, in general, momentarily allowing his passionate qualities to catch the sun. But Clayton's style is remarkable not so much for the notes he plays as for its urgency and sweetness, which are accented by his underscoring vibrato—a vibrato whose light earnestness gives each phrase a stirring, now-I-really-mean-it air. Clayton frequently employs a mute. As opposed to Cootie Williams, who, by constantly waggling his mute about with his hand, emits vowel sounds and windy growls, Clayton keeps his mute tightly in place, producing a distilled version of his open-horn style, in the manner of a man trying to carry on a conversation with his mouth closed.

Berry, on the other hand, has a hustling style, which is, however, no less controlled. Short, round-faced, and wearing the expression of a man peering through a Venetian blind, Berry, despite his restlessness, is even more sparing of notes than Clayton. Berry, who has a hoarse, congested tone, frequently gives the impression of putting the shot, for he delivers his often vibratoless phrases in a heave-ho way that makes him seem far louder than he is. Marvelously adroit at juxtaposing the expected and the unexpected, Berry may play the first half of a chorus in a jabbing, reiterative way, and then, just as one is prepared for a repetition or a slight variation (like Clayton, Berry is primarily an extremely skilled embellisher), he will slip into mountain-goat phrases that leap through a couple of octaves before coming to rest. Nonetheless, Berry has a stubborn, introverted quality, which stems from his mostly seeming to play in a minor key— an effect gained by his frequent use of slightly flatted notes, as though sheer momentum had pushed him past the more conventional ones. Berry, too, often employs a mute, and with tantalizing results. Whereas a mute seems to compound Clayton's lyricism, it conceals Berry's, reducing him to a metallic thrumming.

Clayton and Berry play well in a couple of neo-Basie efforts—"Basie Reunion" (Prestige) and "Songs for Swingers: Buck Clayton with His All-Stars" (Columbia). The first includes such ex-Basie men as Clayton (Berry does not appear in this one), Shad Collins, Paul Quinichette, Jack Washington, and Jo Jones, together with Basie's present bassist, Eddie Jones, and Basie's indefatigable pupil, Nat Pierce. The five numbers, all of them extended, are Basie reruns. The performances, with the exception of Clayton and Jo Jones, who is forced to haul a feet-dragging Pierce after him most of the way, are mixed. Collins is a loose version of Clayton who always seems on the verge of a classic phrase; Quinichette is a staccato duplication of Lester Young; and Washington, a baritone saxophonist who has apparently played only the alto saxophone in late years, sounds impassioned but inexact. Clayton more than makes up for these deficiencies. In the medium-slow "Blues I Like to Hear," he begins in his familiar sidestepping way, pulls himself into the second chorus with a brief growl, and ends up by sailing through the third cho-

Buck Clayton and Emmett Berry

rus with perfectly spaced high notes and an inescapable beat. He takes three comparable choruses in an up-tempo version of "John's Idea." These begin with a break, in which, by fluttering rapidly up and down through a cluster of three notes, like a bird bathing, he sets up an unfaltering tension. During the opening and closing ensembles of "Baby Don't Tell on Me," a slow, rocking blues, Clayton, muted, plays alternately dancing and musing obbligatos behind the other horns, recalling his work behind Paul Robeson in "King Joe," a blues recorded in the early forties with the Basie band, in which Clayton's hollering, from-afar phrases managed to both deflate Robeson's pretentiousness and emphasize the booming, Grand Central Station quality of his voice.

Clayton is joined in the second recording by Berry and such former Basie associates as Dickie Wells, Earl Warren, and Buddy Tate. (The rhythm section, which is adequate, is made up of three men, two of them non-Basie graduates.) There are eight numbers—three blues, three standards, and a couple of Clayton originals. It is Berry, and not the leader, who steals the show, as if Clayton had, out of politeness, deferred to his guest or had simply been bowled over by him. In three numbers— "Swinging at the Copper Rail," "Outer Drive," and "Night Train"—Berry, playing open-horn, performs with an assurance that he has rarely shown on records. Indeed, his two choruses in "Outer Drive," a medium-tempo blues, are close to classic blues improvisations. Tate, a tenor saxophonist who has been celebrating Herschel Evans for a couple of decades, and Warren, an alto saxophonist who switches profitably to clarinet for two numbers, are in good form.

Humph

HUMPHREY LYTTELTON, a thirty-eight-year-old English trumpet player, is his country's most celebrated hot musician. Lyttelton and his eight-man band were in town a week or so ago, preparing for a seventeen-day concert tour through fifteen Eastern cities, to be undertaken with Anita O'Day, and groups headed by George Shearing, Thelonious Monk, Lennie Tristano, and an English colleague, Ronnie Ross. I talked with him on the eve of the tour in a friend's midtown apartment, and discovered him to be a tall (six feet three), ample-waisted man with a high forehead, unruly hair, long sideburns, and a sad-eyed mien that strikingly resembled Claude Rains'. He was wearing a brilliant-blue tie, a gray shirt, and a shapeless gray suit, and he looked tired. "I'm dead," Lyttelton said, reading my thoughts. "I finished being interviewed on the radio by Bea Kalmus at 2 A.M. this morning, and then I ran into Ronnie Ross, and he said, 'Come on, let's go to Eddie Condon's,' and we did, and I had a good long sit-in with the band. It's been that way ever since I arrived, a few days ago. This is my first American visit, and there's so much jazz here that I feel rather like a starving man suddenly confronted with a nine-course meal. I've been to Condon's, the Metropole, and Basie's bar in Harlem, and had an excellent Italian dinner at the Arpeggio with Roy Eldridge blowing in my ear."

How had Lyttelton happened to become a jazz musician? "I had to break the family mold to do it," he replied. "We go back to the twelfth century, and aside from such renegades as myself and the last Humphrey Lyttelton, who got himself hanged, drawn, and quartered for his part in the Gunpowder Plot, we've had nothing but judges, generals, schoolmasters, bishops, and the like. My father, who's seventy-six now, was a professor of English literature at Eton for twenty-five years, and that's where I was raised. I took up the trumpet at fifteen, after hearing Louis Armstrong's first recording of 'Basin Street,' which hit me with terrible force. My mother gave me the money for the trumpet during the annual Eton-Harrow cricket match, which takes place over a weekend in London. I was attending the match in the full school uniform of top hat, colored waistcoat, black-and-white checked trousers, and pale-blue carnation, but after the first few hours I couldn't stand it any longer and took off, top hat and all, for Charing Cross, London's Tin Pan Alley and musical-instrument center. I created quite a stir in the shops. A year later, I had a four-piece band, and for six months we practiced every Sunday afternoon in a room directly beneath my father's study. The only tune we knew was 'Whispering,' and it's the only pop tune my father has ever learned. Then came six years in the Grenadier Guards. I landed at Salerno with a pistol in one hand and my trumpet, wrapped in a sandbag, in the other. After the war, I played the trumpet by night and worked as a cartoonist on the London *Daily Mail* by day. Part of my job was to fill in the dialogue in the balloons of another cartoonist's drawings, which my family regarded as the first serious step in my decline. In 1948, I hit bottom by forming my own band. We've played at the same place in London ever since, and everybody there, waiters included, calls me Humph. We used to play Dixieland, which was very popular. Even the mums and dads liked it, probably because they felt that in any deeper kind of jazz there might be something going on that they'd just as soon not know about. Now we resemble the old Basie band, and we're not as popular any more, but we're happier. I do a lot of writing. I have two music columns in London papers, in which I act as a kind of counter-jazz critic by salving down all the harsh things that other critics say. I've written two books, both auto-biographies, and I do a lot of television work."

Lyttleton interrupted himself with a cavernous yawn, slowly stood up, and asked if I'd like some tomato juice. I said yes, and he fetched two pail-sized glasses, fell back into his chair, and resumed talking. "What English jazz musicians need more than anything else is to hear and play with American musicians. When Armstrong came to England a while back, I heard him twenty-two times. I went to eleven Ellington concerts and twenty-five Basie concerts not long afterward. I regard this tour as the peak of my career. My father, though, regards it philosophically. 'Do what you want, but do it *well*,' he's always told me. Not long ago, he dropped into the night club in London to look around, and the only comment he made was that he'd never seen so many beautiful girls under one roof at one time before. A fine gentleman."

Garner Unveiled

ERROL GARNER is a brilliant deceiver. For well over a decade, his vitality and home-made style have made him appear to a steadily swelling group of admirers as one of the few genuinely gifted modern jazz pianists. But in the past year or two it has become increasingly clear that something sly has been afoot. His celebrated manner of playing—the dense through-the-gloaming introductions, which often turn into complete impressionistic compositions; the Indian-file single-note lines; the leapfrogging octave chords; the thump-thump-thump left-hand figures; the heavily pedaled chordal interludes; the precipitous use of dynamics; the pealing tremolo passages—has seemingly remained the same. Lately, to compound the deception, Garner's style has—because of his undiminished ebullience and his tendency to elaborate on his elaborations—given the impression of an even greater richness. But what has really happened, is that Garner, like many of his colleagues and like many practitioners of whatever art, has been following that subtle and melancholy downward curve that proceeds from freshness, to repetition, to the level where repetition topples over into self-parody. The result is that Garner, no longer a true improviser or even embellisher, now approaches a melody as if it were a hat rack, by draping it with self-caricaturing mannerisms that make even his accompanying vocal effects —"Ayuum," "Me-yes," "Uh-hum"—predictable. The hat rack disappears, but it doesn't change shape.

All this was obvious last Friday at Carnegie Hall, when Garner, accompanied by bass and drums, gave a concert in which his lack of invention was almost completely concealed beneath these mannerisms, which have recently been crowned with a full set of stage gestures—quick standing bows after each number; clusters of nods and head-shakings delivered to his accompanists; encores designed, because of their brevity, to tease instead of satisfy. The tunes Garner chose—there were a couple of dozen in all—were largely taken from his recordings, and included, in addition to some blues and several of his own compositions, such things as "Robbin's Nest," "The Man I Love," "Will You Still Be Mine?," "I Can't Get Started with You," "Love for Sale," "I Love Paris," and "I Didn't Know What Time It Was." None of them lasted for more than half a dozen choruses—in the past, Garner has created improvisations that have lasted as much as eight or nine minutes—and each was pat and premeditated. Garner's accompanists, Eddie Calhoun (bass) and Kelly Martin (drums), played as though they, also, had climbed the same flight of stairs once too often.

Dinosaurs in the Morning

THE best thing that ever happened to jazz—the most evanescent of arts—is the recording machine. Without this means of preservation, the music might simply have bumbled on awhile as a minor facet of American life and then vanished. At that, the countless jazz records made since 1917 represent only a tiny fraction of all the jazz that has been played. Gone forever are such unrecorded events as the Kansas City saxophone bees between Lester Young, Coleman Hawkins, and Ben Webster; the trumpet playing of Buddy Petit, Chris Kelly, and Emmett Hardy; the Chick Webb-Benny Goodman duels at the Savoy Ballroom, in Harlem; the Sunday-afternoon jam sessions at Jimmy Ryan's, at any one of which could be heard Hot Lips Page, Roy Eldridge, Sidney Catlett, James P. Johnson, Frankie Newton, Coleman Hawkins, and Sidney Bechet; the Earl Hines band of 1943, in which Dizzy Gillespie and Charlie Parker were busy fashioning the cornerstone of bebop; and the monumental unaccompanied ten-minute drum solo Catlett took one night at Café Society Uptown just to pass the time until the floor show got underway. Moreover, very little of the enormous amount of jazz that *has* been recorded is satisfactory. The blank, now-or-never atmosphere of the recording studio has unbalanced more than one jazz musician; indeed, such resolute performers as Fletcher Henderson, Bix Beidebecke, and Art Tatum reportedly never came through whole on records.

All this is by way of saying that when one hears the album "Spirituals to Swing" (Vanguard), which has just been released and which contains thirty-one numbers recorded at the two legendary Carnegie Hall concerts presented by John Hammond in 1938 and 1939, it is like getting up one morning, going to the window, and seeing a dinosaur walk by. Landmarks in more ways than one, these concerts helped, because they were played largely by Negroes, to loosen the bars that still prevented Negro jazz musicians from performing in the nation's major entertainment outlets. They brought to wide attention such obscure and valuable performers as Albert Ammons, Pete Johnson, Meade Lux Lewis, Joe Turner, Ida Cox, Big Bill Broonzy, Sidney Bechet, Tommy Ladnier, James P. Johnson, Lester Young, and Charlie Christian. They amounted to a miniature history of jazz that was played, often as not, by its very creators, many of whom are now dead. Finally, they produced some extraordinary music. The selections from the two evenings have been adroitly chosen and arranged; there are few dull spots, and the continuity is full of invigorating changes of pace. Thus, we hear, on the second side, a couple of selections by the Kansas City Six (Buck Clayton, Lester Young, Freddie Greene, Walter Page, and Jo Jones, with Charlie Christian sitting in); a Count Basie piano solo accompanied by Page and Jones; the Kansas City Six again, with Basie instead of Christian; a pair of unaccompanied piano solos by James P. Johnson; and two numbers by Sidney Bechet's New Orleans Feetwarmers, with Ladnier, Johnson, and part of the Basie rhythm section included.

It's almost impossible to single out any person or group from all the delights that occur. Near the head of the list is Christian, who, at the age of twenty, had just joined Benny Goodman, and who, during the two years before his death, was to help put bebop on its feet. Plucked out of Oklahoma by Hammond, who has singlehandedly changed the course of jazz by similarly boosting along Count Basie, Goodman, and Billie Holiday, Christian had a revolutionary style. He was, after Lonnie Johnson, Eddie Lang, Eddie Durham, and Dick McDonough, the first guitarist to explore fully the use of single-string rather than chorded solos. His almost orchestral tone fell between the singsong effect of his predecessors (most of whom, of course, had used the unamplified guitar) and the projectile smoothness of his successors. Although he invariably managed to transmit the emotional fervor behind his work—a difficult accomplishment on a semi-percussive instrument—Christian's playing was utterly relaxed. In a solo, he would often develop a simple, arresting riff figure (many of these riffs eventually reappeared as the melodies of the tunes recorded by the Goodman sextet and septet) for a couple of measures, drop in a short connecting phrase, and, after holding its last note for several beats, tip into a long single-note melodic line that elbowed the limits of conventional jazz harmony and that might continue for eight or more measures and then be capped by another sustained note, which seemed to leave the solo hanging peaceably in midair. Not one of Christian's half-dozen solos is mediocre, and some are stunning. These last occur in "Memories of You," played with the Goodman sextet (Goodman, Christian, Lionel Hampton, Fletcher Henderson, Artie Bernstein, Nick Fatool), and in a slow, affecting blues, "Pagin' the Devil," done with the Kansas City Six, in which Christian takes two choruses, replete with those stopped-motion notes, lanky explorations into the lower registers of the instrument, and graceful in-one-breath melodic lines.

Lester Young, who appears with Christian in three numbers—a one-time union on records that suggests a tête-à-tête between Babe Ruth and Ted Williams—is in equally good form, particularly in "Blues with Helen," where he delivers two choruses on the clarinet. In "Good Morning Blues" and "Pagin' the Devil," he switches to the tenor saxophone and plays so softly he seems to be merely thinking his notes, and in "Don't Be That Way" he takes a remarkable chorus that challenges all his recorded work in the late thirties. Next in line after Young are Pete Johnson and Joe Turner, who do a variation of "Roll 'Em Pete" called "It's All Right Baby." In addition to playing two solo choruses, Johnson provides bustling accompaniment for Turner, who has never, at least on records, been in better voice. There are many more sweets—a rousing solo by James P. Johnson, "Carolina Shout," in which he pits cannonlike left-hand chords against filigreed right-hand figures; another piano solo, "I Ain't Got Nobody," in which Count Basie explicitly and charmingly spells out his debt to Johnson and Fats Waller for two choruses and then slips into two double-time choruses of his own style; Sidney Bechet and Tommy Ladnier attempting to outshout each other (as they had done on their original Feetwarmer sides six years before); a couple of blues by Sonny Terry, who shifts back and forth so rapidly between eerie falsetto singing and his harmonica that the two sounds sometimes seem simultaneous; and Mitchell's Christian Singers, a gospel group, composed of two tenors, a baritone, and a bass, whose subtle and ingenious ensemble singing is full of brownish, grating harmonies and counterpoint. There is one major disappointment on the records. The Count Basie band, at the peak of its powers, appears in only two and a half numbers (a blues, in which it accompanies the trumpet of Hot Lips Page, who was a better blues singer than a trumpeter; a fast, ragged rendition of "Rhythm Man"; and the last three ensemble choruses of "One O'Clock Jump"), which leave one with the feeling, after all, of having got to the window just as the dinosaur was disappearing around the corner.

It is quite possible that the encomiums that appear in the liner notes for two new records by Ornette Coleman, an amazing twenty-nine-year-old alto saxophonist from Texas, and that include such Ciceronian periods as "I'm especially convinced that Ornette Coleman is making a unique and valuable contribution to 'tomorrow's' music" and "I believe that what Ornette Coleman is playing will affect the whole character of jazz music profoundly and pervasively," may, because of their authoritarian ring—let alone the difficulties offered by Coleman's playing—repel as many listeners as they attract. Charlie Parker supplies the central heating for Coleman's style, which, accordingly, is both heretical and traditional. As a radical, Coleman has moved abreast of Charlie Mingus and Cecil Taylor, using a method of nearly free improvisation, in which the chord structure and melody of a tune are only nodded at in his effort to create unfettered rhythmic and harmonic excursions. Thus, after a series of deceptively simple phrases, played in a kind of alter-rhythm to the established beat and discolored here and there with brief atonal sallies, he will suddenly shoot into a couple of ascending yelps —incredibly swift runs whose notes actually seem to be vibrated out of the instrument. This hog-calling device leads to the other side of Coleman's style, which is almost archaic. For Coleman's most adventurous tonal flights appear to be attempts to reproduce on his horn the more passionate inflections of the human voice, which, of course, provided the first model for instrumental jazz. These weird emulations come off best at slow tempos and they are a peculiar and wrenching experience.

The two records under consideration, "Ornette Coleman: 'Tomorrow is the Question!'" (Contemporary) and "Ornette Coleman: The Shape of Jazz to Come" (Atlantic), are uneven. Possibly because of a conventional rhythm team, made up of Percy Heath or Red Mitchell and Shelly Manne, Coleman is in comparatively restrained form on the first record. (Don Cherry, his exact counterpart on cornet, is also on hand.) The best of the nine numbers, all of them by Coleman, are "Lorraine," a slow, chanting dirge, complete with a long, mercurial human-voice run by Coleman that raises the hair on one's neck, and "Turnaround," a comfortable medium-tempo blues. (Coleman's and Cherry's ensembles, which are not unlike Coleman's solos, often make it difficult to decipher just what the melody is, if, indeed, it is a melody at all.) On the second record, a different drummer and bassist come closer to Coleman's own tastes (Cherry is again present), and the results are even more otherworldly. The tempos tend to be faster and the rhythmic foundations are full of steadily shifting twists and turns, with the drums and bass performing decorative-melodic rather than purely percussive roles. These deviations, together with Coleman's bare-ganglion playing, give most of the six numbers, all of them again Coleman's, the air of someone racing down a sidewalk littered with banana peels. However, listen to Coleman; he *is* unique.

Part Two: 1960

Jo Jones, dms.

ONE OF the minor legends of jazz, which has a mythology as busy as the Greeks', credits Jo Jones, the forty-eight-year-old Chicago-born drummer, with singlehandedly setting off, in the late thirties, the revolution in drumming since blown forward by Kenny Clarke, Max Roach, Art Blakey, Philly Joe Jones, and Elvin Jones. This theory holds that Jo Jones was the first drummer to use his bass drum for accents as well as for a timekeeper, the first to shift his other accompanying effects to his cymbals, and, all in all, the first to develop a whistling-in-the-morning attack that made most previous drumming resemble coal rattling down a chute. Nonetheless, several contemporary drummers were doing many of the same things, and not necessarily because they knew Jones's work. (A highly regarded legendizing process in jazz is the convenient device of linking musicians with similar styles. Thus, John Lewis was once firmly informed that he resembled the late Clyde Hart, an economical and original pianist who was an indirect founder of bebop. Lewis replied that he had never heard Hart, in the flesh or on records.) Among these drummers were Chick Webb, whose work on the high-hat and the brushes is among the permanent ornaments of jazz; Alvin Burroughs, an adept, clean, nervous performer, who played as if on springs; O'Neil Spencer, who had much in common with Burroughs; Sidney Catlett, whose cymbal patterns, singular snare accents, and free-floating foot pedal were neater and snappier than Jones's; and Dave Tough, who often implied even more than Jones and whose cymbals, in particular, had a splashing clarity. But any disagreement with the theory about Jones's supposed pioneering is leveled not at him but at his admirers, who, like all jazz appreciators, are full of imagination. One of the handful of irreplaceable drummers, he stands—since Webb, Catlett, Burroughs, Spencer, and Tough are dead and most of the rest of his contemporaries are either inferior or in decline—as the last of a great breed.

One reason for Jones's overglorification as a pioneer was his membership, from 1936 to 1948, in the Count Basie rhythm section, which included —in addition to Basie and Jones—Freddie Greene and Walter Page. This Basie rhythm section was classic proof of the powers of implication, for it achieved its ball-bearing motion through an almost Oriental casualness and indirection, as if the last thing in the world it wanted was to supply rhythm for a jazz band. The result was a deceptive sailing-through-life quality that was, like most magic, the product of hard work and a multi-layered complexity that offered the listener two delightful possibilities: the jointless sound of the unit as a whole, or, if one cared to move in for a closeup, the always audible timbre of each of its components. And what marvelously varied timbres they were! At the top was Basie's piano, which, though most often celebrated for its raindrop qualities, attained its relaxed drive from a skillful pitting of loose right-hand figures against heavy left-hand chords. On the next rung came Greene, a peerless rhythm guitarist, whose Prussian beat, guidepost chords, and aeolian-harp delicacy formed a transparent but unbreakable net beneath Basie. Page, who had a generous tone on the bass and a bushy way of hitting his notes, gave the group much of its resonance, which was either echoed by Jones's foot pedal and snare or diluted by his cymbal work. But the group's steady tension also derived from the way its members counteracted each other's occasional lapses. When Page's sense of dynamics or harmony gave way to overly vibrant or bad notes, Basie might blot them up with his left hand or release a spray of upper-register exclamations. When Greene's perfection seemed tediously precise, Jones's accents or Basie's unpredictability offset it. And when Jones occasionally grew heavy, slowed down, or raised the beat, Page, Basie, and Greene would head resolutely in the opposite direction. Most important, the Basie rhythm section dedicated itself to the proposition that each beat is equal, and, knee-actioned, wiped out both its own bumps and those handed down by all past rhythm sections. Although the group broke up more than a decade ago (only Greene remains with Basie), its low-key drive continues to seep into the four corners of jazz. And Jones, who has since worked with all types of jazz musicians, has been particularly pervasive.

Jones's style, which has not changed appreciably in the past twenty-five years, except for some sporadic, and pardonable, middle-aged heaviness, is elegant and subtle. As an accompanist, he provides a cushion of air for his associates to ride on. Primarily, this is achieved by his high-hat technique. His oarlocks muffled, he avoids the deliberate chunt chunt-chunt effect of most drummers

Jo Jones, dms.

by never allowing the sound of his stick striking the cymbals to be audible, and instead of ceaselessly clapping his cymbals shut on the traditionally accented beats he frequently keeps them open for several beats, producing a shooshing, drifting-downstream quality. Jones's high-hat seems alternately to push a soloist along, to play tag with him, and—in the brief, sustained shooshes—to glide along beside him. His high-hat also varies a good deal according to tempo. At low speeds the cymbals sound like quiet water ebbing. At fast tempos they project an intensity that is the result of precision rather than the increase in volume displayed by most drummers. The rest of the time, Jones carries the beat on a couple of ride cymbals, on which—as opposed to the tinsmith's tink tink-tink of many drummers—he gets a clean, pushing ring. All of Jones's cymbal-playing is contained by spare and irregular accents on the bass drum and the snare, the latter of which he employs for rim shots that give the effect of being fired at the soloist's feet to keep him dancing. On top of all this, these devices form an unbroken flow; each number—pneumatically supported—comes through free of the cracks and breaks that drummers often inflict in the belief that they are providing support. Jones's brushes have been equaled by only a few drummers. They are neat, dry, and full of suggestive snare-drum accents, and when used on cymbals often seem an embellishment of silence rather than a full-blooded sound.

Jones is the embodiment of his own playing. A handsome, partly bald man whose physique resembles a tightly packed cigar and who moves in a quick, restless way, he smiles continually when he is at work, in a radiant, everything-is-fine-at-home fashion. Although he sits very still behind his drums (remember the demonic posturing of Gene Krupa?), his hands, attached to waving undersea arms, flicker about his set and his head snaps disdainfully from side to side, like a flamenco dancer's. His solos, which have recently increased in length and variety but without losing any of their structure, sometimes begin with the brushes, which tick and polish their way between his snare drum and his tom-toms in patterns frequently broken by punching pauses. (Jones's solo brushwork—stinging and nimble—suggests, in sound and figure, that ideal of all tap-dancing, which great tap-dancers always seem headed for but never quite reach.) After a while Jones may joggle his high-hat cymbals up and down with his foot, while switching to drumsticks, and launch into riffling, clicking beats on the rim of a tom-tom as well as on its head (he may muffle it with one hand, achieving the sound produced by kicking a full suitcase), interspersed with sudden free tom-tom booms. He will then drop his sticks, under cover of more high-hat joggling, and go at the tom-toms with his hands, hitting them with a finger-breaking crispness. More high-hat, and he will fall into half time and, sticks in hand again, tackle the snare drum, at which he is masterly, starting with a roll as smooth as hot fudge being poured over marble. Gradually loosening the roll with stuttering accents, he will introduce rim shots—a flow of rolling still intact beneath—spacing them with a breath-catching unevenness, and then, in a boomlay-boom fashion, begin mixing in tom-tom strokes until the tom-toms take over and, in turn, are broken by snippets of snare-drum beats. Jones will slowly subside after returning to the snare for a stream of rapid on-beat strokes, and—an eight-day clock running down— end with a quiet bass-drum thump. There have been no cymbal explosions, repetitions, or dizzying, narcissistic technical displays. One has the feeling, in fact, of having heard distilled rhythm.

Three of Jones's recent efforts—"The Jo Jones Special" (Vanguard), "Jo Jones Trio" (Everest), and "Jo Jones Plus Two" (Vanguard)—are sufficient samplers of his work. The first record is valuable largely for two takes of "Shoe Shine Boy," in which the old Basie rhythm section is reassembled, along with Emmett Berry, Lucky Thompson, and Benny Green. (Nat Pierce is on piano in four of the five other numbers, and for the last there is an entirely different group, composed of—among others—Pete Johnson, Lawrence Brown, and Buddy Tate.) The two versions are done at medium-up tempos, and are just about equal in quality. Thompson and Berry are in commendable form, but the rhythm section is priceless. Listen, in the first take, to the way Jones switches from joyous high-hat work behind Basie's solo to plunging, out-in-the-open patterns on his ride cymbal when the first horn enters; to Basie's down-the-mountainside left hand near the end of Thompson's first chorus; and to Jones's four-bar break on his snare drum at the close of the number, done with sharply uneven dynamics that make the prominent beats split the air. There is also a rendition of "Caravan," by the alternate group, in which Jones takes a tidy solo, complete with mallets on the tom-toms, hands on the tom-toms (here, a plopping sound like that achieved by hooking a finger into one's mouth, closing the lips, and drawing the finger abruptly out), and oil-and-water patterns on the snare with sticks.

Jones is accompanied on the trio records by Ray and Tommy Bryant. Although the first record is crowded with twelve numbers, which seem, because of their brevity (the kind of brevity that smacks of the nervous a.-and-r. man), more like suggestions than complete numbers, there are brilliant instances of Jones's brush work. These occur in a fast blues, "Philadelphia Bound," into which Jones injects some fine high-hat work, particularly behind the bass solo; in the slower "Close Your Eyes," in which his first four-bar break is taken in a startling and absolutely precise double time that conveys to the listener that sense of pleasant astonishment unique to good jazz drumming; and in the leisurely "Embraceable You," in which Jones washes discreetly and ceaselessly back and forth on his snare. On the second trio record, which, surprisingly, is far inferior acoustically to the Everest L.P. (Vanguard's production methods are usually impeccable), Jones develops his "Caravan" solo, in a hundred-miles-an-hour version of "Old Man River," by taking a four-minute excursion in which he uses the brushes, sticks on muffled tom-toms, sticks on open tom-toms, hands on tom-toms, sticks on snare and tom-toms, and a soft ending with sticks on the snare. Jones is exemplary in the remaining eight numbers, both in briefer solos and in his accompaniment. He also allows a good deal of space to Ray Bryant, lending him the same heedless, sparkling force he grants everyone.

Catching Trout

THERE is an unbroken Olympian lineage at the top of jazz—Jelly Roll Morton, Duke Ellington, Count Basie, Thelonious Monk, and John Lewis—which has been distinguished by the curious fact that all its members are composers, arrangers, leaders, and pianists. Monk, however, has added an authentic dimension to the qualities he shares with his colleagues, for he is an almost unparalleled *performer*. Monk is not a vaudevillian in the sense that Louis Armstrong, Dizzy Gillespie, and Gene Krupa are. Instead, he offers the rare spectacle of a man pleasantly and unselfconsciously obsessed by his art. He is, in fact, a transparent, pliable vessel that takes on the shapes, colors, and movements that his emotions, washing against each other within, may dictate on a particular night. A bearish, densely assembled man, with a square head and an oblique face that emits a veiled but unmistakable light, Monk never merely sits at a keyboard. He will hunch his shoulders, elbows akimbo, and knead the keys, bend backward, bring his elbows in, shoot out his forearms, and pluck notes from either end of the keyboard, as if he were catching trout with his bare hands. Then, a giant hammer, he will hit several closely grouped chords, simultaneously jerking his torso. If he is accompanying he may abruptly "lay out" and unconcernedly mop his head, neck, and hands with a flag-size handkerchief, or he may wind his body sinuously from side to side in half time to the beat and, his arms horizontally crooked, slowly snap his fingers—a dancer gracefully illustrating a step in delayed motion. Monk's feet carry on a steady counterpoint. Flattish and nimble, they alternately rustle about beneath the piano, flap convulsively, and dig heel first into the floor. All of this is by way of saying that Monk's five selves were in notable balance early last week, at the most recent of the "Jazz Profiles" concerts.

The affair, held at the Circle in the Square, was

given over entirely to Monk's present quartet, which includes Charlie Rouse, Ron Carter, and Art Taylor. There were eleven numbers, all by Monk, including "Straight No Chaser," "Crepuscule with Nellie," "Well, You Needn't," "Blue Monk," and "Ruby, My Dear," as well as less familiar pieces like "Hackensack," "Epistrophy," and "Ask Me Now." Two infrequently heard Monk compositions—"Monk's Dream" and "Criss-Cross"—were scheduled but never rose to the surface. There were surprises in almost every number. " 'Round Midnight," a ballad with a purplish melody that gives the impression of being too finished for the meddling of improvisation (Monk himself generally sticks close to its melody in his solos), was taken at a jogging double time, which stripped it of some of its stateliness. In "Well, You Needn't," done in a medium tempo, Monk offered an exceptional display of his accompanying technique behind Rouse. He started with offbeat melodic chords, changed to dissonant chords that climbed steadily and slowly up and down the keyboard, released acrid single notes in the upper registers, splattered a chord with his right elbow, and then, falling silent, began one of his Balinese dances. His backing here suggested that he was using Rouse's work as a soft clay on which to record his thoughts; elsewhere, he seemed to be rubbing pleasurably against the grain of Rouse's playing. "Crepuscule with Nellie," a slow hymn-lullaby, received tantalizing treatment. The first chorus was played straight by the group, and then, with the audience prepared for improvisation, the number ended. "Blue Monk" was taken at a medium-fast tempo instead of its usual slow rock, and thus paved the way for the closing numbers, "Hackensack" and "Rhythm-n-ing," two steam baths that left the audience at that exquisite point between satisfaction and wanting more at which all audiences should be left. Monk is a master of this art— in the way he measures his solos, his numbers, and even whole concerts.

Something Else

A SINGULAR EVENT took place last week, when Baby Laurence, the semi-legendary jazz tap dancer, opened at the Showplace, a second-story cave on West Fourth Street. Indeed, Laurence's opening set was one of those claps of brilliance that are seemingly over before they have begun. Working on a stage the size of a billiard table Laurence danced only two numbers, which, taken together, lasted well under ten minutes, but which were of such intensity that they appeared to be a telescoping of all tap dancing. Laurence was discreetly backed in the first number by Charlie Mingus, Roland Hanna (piano), and Danny Richmond. After some purposely heavy, flat-footed introductory steps in medium tempo, Laurence shot into double time, pausing repeatedly and suddenly for short triple-time passages, done as breaks, that were compounded of a startling variety of accents, not one of which was missed, and that invariably came out just right. These seesaw patterns were followed by abrupt slow shufflings, which gave way to offbeats against a backboard, and then to irregular, out-of-rhythm scrapings carried out on three shallow steps on one side of the stage. More breaks, a few crackling spins, and the dance was over. The shorter second number was a solo. It consisted of half a dozen rhythms—including a military beat—that, flawlessly juxtaposed, proved that what Laurence is, essentially, is a great drummer. As such, he did, in a matter of minutes, what Fred Astaire and Gene Kelly have only dreamed of.

I caught up with Laurence later in the evening and asked him how his engagement had come about. "Marshall Stearns, the jazz writer, helped me get the job," Laurence, a short, slim, dapper man with gray-streaked hair, told me. "He'd interviewed me for a book he's doing on jazz dancing, and he suggested I come here to the Showplace, where Mingus puts on informal dance sessions on Thursday nights. So I did, I danced, and Mingus said, 'Baby, you want a job, I'll fire my piano player who's always late anyway and hire you.' I'm very lucky, you know. Between the entertainment tax and the Hollywood and Broadway producers, who use nothing but what we call choreography dancing, there just aren't many jobs for jazz dancers."

Laurence pulled a pack of du Mauriers out of his pocket, and I lit one for him. "Dancing was an accident I fell into," he continued. "I started as a Bobby Breen-type singer in Baltimore late in 1932, when I was twelve. I worked with McKinney's Cotton Pickers over at College Park, and one day Don Redman's band come to town, and he heard me sing and asked my mama could he hire me and take me on the road. My mama told him, 'Get him a tutor, provide him an education, and he can go.' Well, Redman did, and I was on the road with him for about a year. Then my mother died, and I went home and joined my brother in a vocal group, the Four Buds, and we went up to New York. We accompanied ourselves on the ukulele and did some dancing, too, and that's when I started to learn.

Something Else   71

We worked at Dickie Wells's place in Harlem, and he kind of adopted me. I was born Laurence Donald Jackson, and he gave me my professional name. Then I started going over to the Hoofer's Club, where all the dancers hung out. Harold Mablin began teaching me there. He gave me the devil because I turned all his steps around, and pretty soon he just gave me ideas and I went on from there. In a year, I was really dancing. I don't know how I did it. It was just one of those things. I jobbed around Harlem and Cincinnati and Washington, and in the late thirties I joined a group called the Three Gobs. We got on the bill at the Apollo, but the manager didn't want us in sailor suits, so he dressed us up in kilts and called us the Merry Scotchmen. We stopped the show. Then we went into Kelly's Stable, downtown. We accompanied ourselves and sang Jimmie Lunceford arrangements in five-part harmony, and it was something else. Around 1940, I started doing a single—just dancing. I worked with Rochester at the Apollo. I opened the show, and I broke it up. Nobody wanted to come on after me—the band, which was the Savoy Sultans, Rochester, no one—so they put me at the end of the bill. I did a couple of coffee concerts at the Museum of Modern Art, and traveled with Count Basie and Duke Ellington until the entertainment tax came along and things got hard." Laurence sighed, pulled a long face, and fell silent. "After that, I began running with a fast crowd and got sick. I pretty much stopped dancing. I learned the guitar and started singing again, and I even wrote poetry. I got married in 1953, and my wife kept after me and started me dancing again."

I asked Laurence who had taught him most.

"I've learned from everybody," he said.

"Dancers like John Bubbles and Teddy Hale. Hale got a sound—Lord, what a sound! He died last year. And dancers like Eddie Rector and Pete Nugent and Honi Coles and Toots Davis and Jack Wiggins. I learned from Art Tatum, too. I worked with him on Fifty-second Street, and I tried to duplicate his sound with my feet. I did the same thing rhythmically when Charlie Parker came along. Maybe I've learned most from drummers, though. One time I was on the television show Eddie Condon had in the forties. There was Buddy Rich, Teddy Hale, Milt Buckner, and me, and we each took a chorus, then we started swapping eight-bar breaks, then four-bar breaks, then two. It was something else. I've worked with Max Roach, and we trade ideas. I'm learning right now from Mingus. I'm also inventing new solo routines. Last week, I stumbled onto something I call 'An Afternoon in Percussion,' which is supposed to sound like a jazz drummer practicing at home in the afternoon and driving his neighbors wild. But I have a dream. I'd like to give a concert in Carnegie Hall and get all the great jazz tap dancers and let the people see what they've been missing these past ten, twelve years. People should know. It's a beautiful art. I'd get everybody from uptown—Bubbles and Nugent and Coles—and a boy works in Cincinnati who's never been to New York named Ground Hog. He's a little, short, homely-looking stud, but when he dances you forget that. The people should know about Ground Hog and all the rest. They should see what they've been missing all these years."

Something Else

Miss Holiday

Toward the end of her life, Billie Holiday, who died last summer, at the age of forty-four, had become inextricably caught in a tangle of notoriety and fame. It was compounded of an endless series of skirmishes with the police and the courts (she was shamelessly arrested on her deathbed for the alleged possession of narcotics); the bitter, vindictive, self-pitying image of herself established in her autobiography, published in 1956—a to-hell-with-you image that tended to repel rather than attract compassion; and the fervent adulation still granted her by a diminishing but ferocious band of admirers. Her new listeners must have been puzzled by all this turmoil, for she sang during much of the fifties with a heavy, unsteady voice that sometimes gave the impression of being pushed painfully in front of her, like a medicine ball. She seemed, in fact, to be embattled with every song she tackled. Nonetheless, her admirers were not mad. Between 1935, when she popped out of nowhere, and 1940, Miss Holiday had knocked a good portion of the jazz world on its ear with a hundred or so recordings, several dozen of which rank with the greatest of non-classical vocal efforts. Part of the success of these recordings, which have an uncanny balance of ease, control, unself-consciousness, emotion, and humor, is due to the accompaniment provided by small bands made up of men like Lester Young, Buck Clayton, Roy Eldridge, Benny Goodman, and Teddy Wilson. Though their work—in obbligatos that underline the grace of her voice, in exemplary solos, and in tumbling, laughing ensembles—often takes up as much space as the vocals, it is Miss Holiday who continues to astonish.

Until she appeared, genuine jazz singing had been practiced largely by a myriad of often obscure blues singers led by Bessie Smith, and by a handful of instrumentalists led by Louis Armstrong. Bessie Smith leveled a massive lyricism at limited materials, while Armstrong's coalyard rumblings, though irresistible in themselves, occasionally seemed to have little to do with singing. Distilling and mixing the best of her predecessors with her own high talents, Billie Holiday became the first full-fledged jazz singer (and, with the defection in recent years of Ella Fitzgerald and Sarah Vaughan, possibly the last). She could sing anything, and her style was completely her own. She appeared to *play* her voice rather than sing with it. In addition to a hornlike control of melody and rhythm, she had an affecting contralto that took on innumerable timbres: a dark-brown sound, sometimes fretted by growls or hoarseness, in the lower register; a pliable oboe tone in the high register; and a clear, pushing, little-girl alto in between. Her style came in three subtly different parts. There was one for ephemeral popular songs, one for the more durable efforts of George Gershwin and his peers, and one for the blues. Since she was primarily an improviser, not an interpreter, she was often most striking when handling pop songs, like "Yankee Doodle Never Went to Town," "It's Too Hot for Words," and "What a Little Moonlight Can Do," which she spattered with a mocking, let's-have-some-fun-with-this air. Thus, at a fast tempo, she might loll back in half time, and not only elongate each word, so that it seemed nothing but vowels, but flatten the melody into a near-monotone of four or five notes. Then, in the last eight bars or so, she would suddenly pounce on the beat, pick up the melody, and close in a here-I-am rush. (If the evil was in her she might stomp such a number all the way through, rocking it relentlessly back and forth and coating it with dead-serious growls.) At slow tempos, she would use the full range of her voice, adding exaggerated smears to her phrases or dotting them with series of laughlike staccato notes. At the same time, she was busy fashioning a deceptively simple and thorough melodic variation on the tune, smoothing its wrinkles, toughening up its soft spots, and lending it far more lyricism than it usually deserved. This was accomplished not by superimposing melodic candelabra on her material, in the manner of Sarah Vaughan and her baroque students, but by unobtrusively altering its melodic and rhythmic structure with a flow of marvelously placed phrases that might wander around behind the beat, and then suddenly push ahead of it (each syllable urgently pinned to a staccato note) or slide through legato curves full of blue notes and generous vibratos. Miss Holiday's rhythmic sense had much in common with Lester Young's, who would sooner have gone into another line of work than place a note conventionally. Moreover, her enunciation of pop songs was a mixture of clarity and caricature, bringing into action that rule of ridicule that the victim be reproduced perfectly before being destroyed. Her "moon"'s and "June"'s rang like bells, and one didn't hear their cracks until the sound began to die away. The composers of the pop songs she sang should be grateful; her renditions ("Ooo-ooo-ooo/ What a lil moonlaight can do-oo-oo"), and not the songs, are what we remember.

Her approach to Gershwin and such was almost reverent in comparison. In a number like "Summertime," she allowed the emotion that she had spent on lesser materials in sarcasm or near-flippancy to come through undisguised. Ceaselessly inventive, she would still shape the melody to fit her voice and mood, but in such a way that its beauties—and not hers—were pointed up. (The number of popular singers, to say nothing of jazz singers, who have been able to slip inside their material, instead of plodding along beside it, is remarkably small.) "Summertime" became a pure lullaby, "But Not for Me" a self-joshing lament, and "Porgy" a prayer. When there were superior lyrics on hand, she underlined them with a diction and an understanding that shunted the meaning of each word forward. More than that, she would, at her best, lend a first-rate song a new and peculiarly heightened emotion that, one suddenly realized, its composer had only been reaching for. And the effort never showed.

Miss Holiday simply let go when she sang the blues. She was never, however, a loud singer, nor did she depend on the big whisper of most of her microphone-reared successors; instead, she projected her voice firmly, keeping in steady balance her enunciation, timbre, and phrasing. She was, in fact, a model elocutionist. Free of the more complex structures of the standard popular song, she moved through the innumerable emotional pastures of the form, ranging from the down-and-out to the joyous to the nasty and biting to quiet, almost loving blues.

Then, in 1944, when Miss Holiday started recording again (after the recording bans), the magic had begun to vanish. Perhaps it was the increasing strain of her private life, or the mysterious rigor mortis that so often freezes highly talented but untrained and basically intuitive performers. At any rate, she had become self-conscious. Although her voice had improved in resonance and control, her style had grown mannered. She ended her phrases with disconcerting, lachrymose dips. She struggled with her words instead of batting them about or savoring them. The melodic twists and turns lost their spontaneity. One could accurately predict her rhythmic patterns. Even her beauty—the huge gardenia clamped to the side of her head; the high, flashing cheekbones; the almost motionless body, the snapping fingers, and the thrown-back head; the mobile mouth, which seemed to measure the emotional shape and texture of each word—implied careful calculation. From time to time, some of this stylization lifted—she never, of course, lost her *presence*, which became more and more melancholy —and there were glimpses of her old naturalness. After 1950, her voice grew deeper and coarser, and her sense of pitch and phrasing eluded her, and finally she became that most rending of spectacles —a once great performer doing a parody of herself that could have been bettered by her inferiors. Her still devoted partisans clamored on; they would have done her greater service by doffing their hats and remaining silent.

Miss Holiday's most recent records chronicle her work from 1944 until a year or two before her death. Among them are "An Evening with Eddie Heywood and Billie Holiday" (Commodore), "The Billie Holiday Story" (Decca), and "The Unforgettable Lady Day" (Verve). By and large, they proceed steadily and sadly downward. The first record includes four Holiday numbers—three standards and a blues—that were done in 1944. (The rest are instrumentals by Eddie Heywood's small band, which also provides her accompaniment.) The best of them is a slow blues, "I Love My Man," in which, dropping her mannerisms, she nearly equals her classic rendition of another blues, "Fine and Mellow," recorded five years before. The Decca collection brings together twenty-four numbers—most of them standards—recorded between 1944 and 1950, and it varies sharply in quality. The accompaniment runs from the indifferent to the stifling. Nevertheless, in numbers like "Lover Man," "I'll Look Around," "Deep Song," "My Man," "Good Morning, Heartache," and "Solitude," she sings in her best forties style.

The Verve album, which consists of twenty-three standards recorded between 1949 and 1957 with a variety of small groups made up of such men as Ben Webster, Harry Edison, Charlie Shavers, Oscar Peterson, and Benny Carter, begins—give or take a little overlapping—where the Decca set stops. There are some valuable things. Six of the numbers were set down at a concert in 1949 on the West Coast, and Miss Holiday sings throughout with an ease and confidence that result in two first-rate efforts—a medium-slow "Man I Love," which ranks with any of her work in the forties, and a fresh, peaceful "All of Me." The eleven numbers from 1952 are not far behind; the notable ones are slow versions of "I Can't Face the Music" and "These Foolish Things." The cracks begin to show in the two 1954 numbers, and then, amazingly, there is a medium-tempo "Please Don't Talk About Me When I'm Gone," done a year later, in which Miss Holiday magically reverts to the late thirties, delivering the first chorus in a light, bantering, husky voice that is memorable. ("When Your Lover Has Gone," apparently made at the same session, is, nevertheless, curiously heavy and uncertain.) With the exception of the last chorus of a 1957 "Gee Baby, Ain't I Good to You," in which Miss Holiday virtually rocks herself into effective shape, the rest of the album is rewarding only for the accompaniment of Webster and Edison. But one is cheered by the recent news that Columbia is considering reissuing the best of the 1935–40 Holiday sides hidden away in its vaults. It would be inhuman not to.

R.I.P.

THE APPEARANCE OF "The Real Boogie Woogie: Memphis Slim, Piano Solos" (Folkways Records) is a surprising event; it is the first new boogie-woogie record to be released in nearly a decade, and, more than that, its title tells the truth. An all but vanished art, boogie-woogie remains, in recordings and in the memory, one of the milestones of jazz. A complex, incandescent solo-piano music whose thematic material was restricted almost wholly to the twelve-bar blues, it embraced, because of its variety and power, all the emotional shades of the blues. Its obvious features have been widely celebrated and widely misunderstood. Unlike the rest of jazz piano, which depends largely on the right hand, boogie-woogie was a two-part, two-handed contrapuntal music that collapsed if either hand was undeveloped. It was also a basically rhythmic and harmonic form that only nodded at melodic invention. The left hand was chiefly characterized by the *ostinato* bass. This bass was often composed of dotted eighth or dotted sixteenth notes, and it included "walking" basses, "rolling" basses, heavy staccato basses, and spare four-four basses often tinged with Spanish rhythms. (Contrary to general belief, only a few boogie-woogie basses had eight beats to the bar.) A boogie-woogie pianist might use the same bass through an entire chorus or a succession of choruses, but more often he changed basses, and sometimes even registers, once in each chorus. The monotonous rumble popularly associated with boogie-woogie was an illusion; close attention revealed a constant flow of new colors. The right hand was even freer. The pianist might use legato or staccato arpeggios, a single note struck lackadaisically throughout a whole chorus, tremolos of various speeds, chorded or single-note riffs, simple, fragmentary melodic lines, and clusters of chords that frequently absorbed single-note melodies or dissolved into them. Occasionally one rhythm popped up, simultaneously in the bass and treble, but generally the right hand went its own way, setting up a welter of cross-rhythms that sometimes shifted from measure to measure. Added to all this was an intuitive harmonic sense that ranged from single or multivoiced melodies to dissonances. Boogie-woogie was a polyphonic, polyrhythmic, and at times even polytonal music.

It is often regarded primarily as a stomp music. Nonetheless, it was played at every speed. There were tempos that were so slow they were tempoless. Numbers played this way became a collection of sorrowful, introverted reflections on the blues that have rarely been surpassed for unadulterated sadness. The brighter the tempo, the more effulgent the music; at medium-slow or medium speeds, the lyrical content was perfectly balanced by its rhythmic aspects. Many of the "train" pieces—Meade Lux Lewis's "Honky Tonk Train Blues" is the most famous—were played in these tempos, and they provided extended musical images that caught perfectly the concatenation of sounds, motion, and force of steam-hauled trains. They also caught the emotions of transition that trains so peculiarly symbolize. Fast boogie-woogie was a rock-breaking wonder. A distillation of hurry and strength, it was one of the few forms of jazz with a climactic structure. In a fast number, melodic repetition and the compounding of various rhythms gradually took on a solidity that had no breathing spaces and that reached an impressive intensity in the closing choruses. Not many other types of music have offered such a sense of rampage. And yet, despite its turbine quality, fast boogie-woogie never lost the essential plaintiveness of the blues. Slow boogie-woogie was a carefully arranged array of still shots; fast boogie-woogie transposed those stills into a motion picture.

The history of boogie-woogie is blurred, romantic, and short. So far as is known, the form was invented around the turn of the century in the Midwest and scattered areas of the South by itinerant laborer-musicians. Its singular percussiveness was probably the result of attempts by its pioneers to overcome, through sheer volume, both inferior instruments and the noisy environment—dances, lumber camps, rent parties, and the like—in which they played. Its repetitiveness and wayward harmonies, which were eventually handled with considerable intelligence, grew out of plain ineptitude.

(For all its supposed "primitiveness," boogie-woogie has never been mastered by a schooled, technically finished pianist.) The music was largely unknown until the late thirties, when it suddenly became a national fad. Every swing band had at least one boogie-woogie arrangement, while one band—Will Bradley's—made a career out of it. Correspondence-course pianists played it at parties. José Iturbi made an unbelievable two-sided 78-r.p.m. boogie-woogie record. The term became widely and genially mispronounced. (Both words rhyme, more or less, with "bookie," rather than "bootie.") The results were ironic and disastrous. The unwieldy complexities and fire of the form, untouched by this imitative army, settled to the bottom, leaving a vapid, colorless liquid. At the same time, the handful of genuine boogie-woogie pianists who abruptly achieved fame and fortune were forced by overexposure to mechanize a fundamentally instinctive music. The craze had vanished by the end of the Second World War, and so, to all intents and purposes, had boogie-woogie itself. Two of its leading exponents, Albert Ammons and Jimmy Yancey, died not long after, while two others, Meade Lux Lewis and Pete Johnson, dropped into obscurity. No reputable neophytes appeared. The music began to be looked down on as ungainly and shallow.

Although there must have been hundreds of proficient boogie-woogie pianists in the twenties and thirties, only Yancey, Ammons, Lewis, and Johnson left a sizable and first-rate body of work behind them. Jimmy Yancey, who died in 1951, at the age of fifty-seven, was, in addition to being a model for Ammons and Lewis, possibly the greatest of all blues pianists. A small, lean, shy man who gave up music professionally in the twenties and took a job as a groundkeeper for the Chicago White Sox, Yancey had a style of classic simplicity. He invented a wide selection of discreet, almost tentative basses that were often set in four-to-the-bar or Spanish-tinged rhythms. His right hand was similarly understated. It rarely left the middle registers, and was limited to elementary chords, loose tremolos, and, principally, to lucid, reiterated melodic figures grouped around or below middle C. He had a sure sense of dynamics, and never went above brisk medium tempos, favoring slow speeds, which gave him the time to wring the maximum amount of emotion from his notes. Indeed, the best of his slow blues—"Death Letter Blues," "Five O'Clock Blues," and "35th and Dearborn"—are indelible. Ammons, Lewis, and Johnson were altogether different from Yancey. In their heyday, in the early forties, all three swelled to tremendous girths, and all three played with a rococo fury that made Yancey seem schoolmasterish. Lewis was the most accomplished of the three. He was adept at all speeds and was perhaps the most complex of all boogie-woogie pianists. His variety of basses was limitless, and so were his right-hand figures. Yancey's influence was clear, but it had been transformed into a fatter, nimbler, more intense approach. Ammons was at once a looser and even more driving pianist. At leisurely tempos, he seemed to spread slowly, like a stain, occasionally slipping out of the confines of boogie-woogie altogether to play a straight stride bass and heavily pedaled right-hand chords. At up tempos, though, he generated a passion that was bent wholly to the rhythmic characteristics of the music. Johnson was a Kansas City-trained pianist who frequently used a walking bass. His slow pieces often resembled Ammons's, but at fast tempos—despite his mountainous walking basses and his agile staccato right-hand chords— he achieved only a tight, dispassionate quality. Johnson's work had more bark than bite. Both Lewis and Johnson have recorded in the past decade, but, sadly, their inventiveness is gone. One hears only repetitions of old phrases, mixed here and there with intimations of their old ingenuity.

Memphis Slim, a forty-five-year-old performer whose real name is Peter Chatman, stands within and without the Yancey tradition. He has obviously listened to Yancey, Ammons, and Lewis, but there are also distinct overtones of lesser-known and less adept pianists like Roosevelt Sykes, Speckled Red, and Cow Cow Davenport. The jostling of these influences is absorbing, notwithstanding Slim's fluffed notes, uncertain time and tonality, and choruses of carelessly varied lengths. The record includes fourteen blues, three of them outstanding. (Slim sings the two vocals on the record in a rich, liquid voice.) The first, ".44 Blues," has a slurred, delayed-action bass that suggests Spanish rhythms, while the right hand plays a stream of staccato chords. "Down Home Blues" is the essence of slow blues. It is so slow it has no beat, and is largely a mass of sonorous, viscous sounds that creep back and forth between an attenuated Yancey-like bass and right-hand chords broken by wild arpeggios. The Spanish rhythms reappear in "Roll and Tumble," which is in a medium-slow tempo and has a rolling bass that here and there is replaced by on-the-beat chords that lend the piece a mock-martial air. The rest of the numbers, though valuable, are uneven. Nonetheless, Memphis Slim comes close to persuading us that he is not, after all, merely vestigial.

R.I.P.   85

Gypsy

THERE HAVE BEEN countless jazz guitarists but, peculiarly, only two masters of the instrument—Charlie Christian and Django Reinhardt (1910–53). They rise from a plain of mediocre-to-good colleagues, including the early blues singer-guitarists, ingenuous performers who tended to reflect their make-do singing in their playing; contemporaries, or near-contemporaries, like Lonnie Johnson, Eddie Lang, Teddy Bunn, Eddie Durham, Al Casey, and Jimmy Shirley; and, since the Second World War, a swarm of young, predominantly white guitarists who, though technically gifted, are almost puzzlingly jejune players. Among these are Barney Kessel, Tal Farlow, Jimmy Raney, Jim Hall, Barry Galbraith, Herb Ellis, and Billy Bauer. (There have been several distinguished non-solo rhythm guitarists, like Freddie Greene, Freddie Guy, Allan Reuss, and Eddie Condon.) The guitar, which gradually replaced the less subtle banjo in the twenties, is, to be sure, a tricky instrument. Both melodic and percussive, it is, in its unamplified form, capable only of distilled colors, and it transmits emotion in an indirect, elusive manner. As a result, it has had a strange career in jazz; no one has ever known quite where it belongs. The pioneer New Orleans, Chicago, and Kansas City musicians used it, if at all, as a rhythm instrument, and it was not until the late twenties, when Johnson and Lang arrived, that the instrument became a promising solo vehicle. A decade later, Reinhardt and Christian were in full flower, along with Bunn, Shirley, et al., and it was by then a fairly important voice in small swing ensembles. The electric amplifier had also been widely adopted, but instead of widening the instrument's tonal possibilities it superimposed a blurred, neon sound that hid the deficiencies of its more inept practitioners and diffused the work of its abler ones. Only Christian seemed able to break through this aural padding; Reinhardt, who began using an amplifier in the forties, never was. Because of its added resonance, many big bands promoted the electric guitar from a rhythm to a solo status, and one guitarist, Alvino Rey, who played in an *aloha* fashion, even became a band leader. Then the big bands began to vanish, bebop advanced its technical complexities and its demand for immediately accessible, one-dimensional sounds, and the guitar, together with the clarinet and the trombone, slipped into semi-obscurity, only to be rescued in the early fifties by its new adherents, who use it with chamber groups that for the most part move on the fringes of jazz. Partly because of their great talents and partly because they have had no successors, Christian and Reinhardt still sound astonishingly up-to-date. Perhaps that's why Capitol Records—a company that, though it generally ignores jazz, guiltily bestirs itself once a decade and produces something lasting—has just brought out "The Best of Django Reinhardt," a set of reissues of twenty-four recordings made in France between 1937 and 1945.

Reinhardt was an uncommon jazz musician. A gypsy born in Belgium, he began playing jazz in France in the early thirties, bringing to the medium all of the quavering, emotional and highly melodic qualities in Central European folk music. This infusion added a striking dimension to his work, which weakened only in his last years, when he began awkwardly investigating the possibilities of bebop. In addition, Reinhardt is the only European jazz musician who can be compared favorably with top-rank American performers. (He came to this country just once, in 1946, after his best days were over, and made a short, unsuccessful tour with Duke Ellington.) His recording career was equally unconventional. Most of his records were made in France with small groups like the Quintet of the Hot Club of France, a unit which he founded in 1934 and which included the unusual instrumentation of violin, solo guitar, two rhythm guitars, and bass. The Quintet, which retained pretty much the same instrumentation and personnel until the war, surmounted its sweetish, salonlike texture and provided Reinhardt with a devoted setting. At the same time, Reinhardt made a couple of dozen frequently remarkable pickup recordings with visiting American musicians like Coleman Hawkins, Benny Carter, Bill Coleman, Shad Collins, Dickie Wells, Barney Bigard, and Rex Stewart. Reinhardt, challenged by hearing jazz straight from the horse's mouth, often surpassed himself, while Wells, Coleman, and Stewart, similarly exercised, set down some of their best solos. (A handsome, mustached, footloose man, Reinhardt was never, unlike many of his worshipful European colleagues, intimidated by his American peers. In 1939, he characteristically turned up late and without a guitar for a session with Stewart and Bigard. An instrument with a broken back was found, and the records were made. Reinhardt never sounded better.) His postwar recordings did not match his earlier efforts, but that doesn't matter. He had already achieved permanence.

Reinhardt had an extraordinary technique (despite two useless, fire-crippled fingers on his left hand), flawless phrasing, taste, and a delicate, luminous tone that left threadlike traceries on the air. The less definable gypsy elements in his work were equally important. Thus, when he improvised, Reinhardt never constructed a solo merely by adding notes to or subtracting them from the chords of a tune—an approach that might or might not result in *melodic* invention. Instead, he seemed to extract the melodic possibilities from a number and convert them into lyrical excursions that had the air of folk melodies. This effect was intensified by his phrasing and by the way he struck his notes. He often appeared to *enter* them. He might approach a sustained note softly, make it swell, hold this expansion for a second, and pass on, letting the note casually taper off into the wavering, questioning sound that served as his vibrato. It was an almost fernlike sound—intricate and fragile. He might tick other notes off quietly, and then, with his unerring dynamics, plunge into louder, more intense, but never fuzzy passages made up of single-note melodic lines or chords that were either hit sharply on the offbeat and tightly cut off at their ends or built into flashing arpeggios. Antedating Charlie Christian, he used a good many notes that gave the impression of being pushed as far as they could go before going flat, and he also employed long, singsong phrases that Christian, Charlie Parker, and Dizzy Gillespie were soon to parallel. In a typical slow or medium-tempo solo—the speed in which his style was most comfortable—he might start with a three-note phrase, placing the first two notes close together and isolating the third an octave or so higher. He would allow the last one to bend into a blue tone, then begin a repetition of the phrase.

Before finishing it—Reinhardt's phrases often seemed to overlap, like shingles—he'd start a quick, ascending figure, break it off, float down through an arpeggio, and pause to let all this settle into his listeners' ears. Next, he would open an extended, melodic, yet almost monotone single-note passage, interspersed with barely struck notes, definitive staccato ones, and sliding effects, end it with an offbeat chord, insert a momentary space, then go into swift chords played staccato or even in a shuffle rhythm, and, returning to a brief single-note figure, close the solo with an even tremolo passage. Reinhardt was also a valuable rhythm guitarist, frequently resembling two or three guitarists playing in unison. He'd use steady onbeat chords, cantering shuffle rhythms, and resounding drumlike offbeats —a device that he probably developed because he played in many drumless groups—or else sudden fortissimo tremolos when the musician he was supporting appeared to need remedial vibrations.

The material in the Capitol album could have been even better. Fifteen of the numbers are by the Hot Club Quintet, five are from the Stewart-Bigard date, there is a 1945 big-band number, one selection done with Bill Coleman and Dickie Wells, one done with Wells, and a curious rendition of the "Bolero," played by an expanded version of the Quintet. However, it is too bad that the big-band effort, the "Bolero," and some of the Hot Club sides, which, when heard consecutively, sound a lot alike, were not sacrificed for the half-dozen superb sessions Reinhardt did with Coleman and/or Wells and which included "Bugle Call Rag," "Hangin' Around Boudon," "The Bill Coleman Blues," and "I Got Rhythm." These are, by and large, invaluable recordings, and they have not been available in this country for many years. The most notable things in the album are "Japanese Sandman" (the number with Wells and Coleman), the slow "Big Boy Blues," a classic number, made with Coleman and the New Orleans clarinetist Frank Goudie (or Goodie, according to most discographies), and the Stewart-Bigard numbers, which are rounded out by the bassist Billy Taylor (not related to the pianist). Among these are "Finesse," a moody slow number, and "Solid Old Man," a slow blues that has possibly the finest solo Rex Stewart has recorded. The Hot Club numbers are practically as good. This group had Stéphane Grappelly on violin, Reinhardt as solo and rhythm guitar, Joseph Reinhardt (Django's brother) and Roger Chaput as rhythm guitars, and Louis Vola on bass. There is an airy, respectful rendition of "Solitude"; a medium-tempo "When Day Is Done" with a two-chorus half-time solo by Reinhardt that amounts to an encyclopedia of his style; Reinhardt's chugging chords in the opening of his solo in "Runnin' Wild"; a "Liebestraum No. 3" that turns into a fine "Basin Street Blues"; and "Minor Swing," which includes a virtuoso display by Reinhardt. It's a pity Reinhardt didn't choose to spend any time in this country when he was at the peak of his powers. He might have altered the course of the jazz guitar.

Historic

THOUGH JAZZ and classical music have been living side by side for forty years, until recently it was classical music—in the form of Stravinsky, Milhaud,

Ravel, Satie, Křenek, and Copland—that did all the running across the yard to borrow a cup of this and a pinch of that. These borrowings included rhythms, minor structural devices, improvisation, the blue note, and the all but inimitable timbres of jazz. During the past ten years or so the practice has become two-way, for jazz has begun adopting the forms, the harmonies, and the instrumentation of classical music, and even its discipline. This neighborliness has grown out of distinct needs. Much modern classical music has dry rot, and the exuberance and fearlessness of the best contemporary jazz offer a possible cure—on the presupposition, of course, that improvisation is a defensible musical form. (Perhaps the chief appeal of genuine jazz improvisation lies in its ability to supply the listener in a matter of moments with an emotional and aesthetic sustenance comparable to that provided by the heavier arts—a peculiarly valuable ability in this split-second age.) At the same time, the finished techniques of many modern jazz musicians have forced them to look abroad for more challenging forms, harmonies, and rhythms. Nevertheless, it is obvious that the set designs of classical music cannot swallow the fluidity of jazz, and vice versa, or each will simply turn into the other. But there is a possible compromise—a new music consisting of the most durable elements of both—and it already has its first prophet. He is Gunther Schuller, a young classical composer and French-horn player with wide experience in modern jazz. For the past three or four years, Schuller has been vigorously stumping for his vision, and last week, at the final "Jazz Profiles" concert, held at the Circle in the Square, he presented the first program devoted entirely to this new music.

There were seven compositions, all by Schuller, who conducted. The music was played jointly by three groups, which, give or take a few musicians, remained onstage throughout. Present were the Contemporary String Quartet (Charles Treger, Joseph Schor, John Garvey, and Joseph Tekula), the Bill Evans Trio (Bill Evans, piano; Scott La-Faro, bass; and Paul Cohen or Sticks Evans, drums), and six ringers (Ornette Coleman, alto saxophone; Eric Dolphy, alto saxophone, flute, clarinet, or bass clarinet; Buell Neidlinger, bass; Barry Galbraith, guitar; Eddie Costa, vibraphone; and Robert DiDomenica, flute). The opening number, "Little Blue Devil"—part of a symphonic work that was given its premiére earlier this year—was hardly more than a cough-quieter, in which patches of strings, a flute solo, and a regular beat were bandied about. But it readied one for the next piece, the new "Variants on a Theme of Thelonious Monk," which Schuller introduced as a set of four variations on Monk's "Criss-Cross." In the first part, taken at a medium tempo, Coleman and Dolphy, on alto saxophone, stated the melody, and then Coleman soloed, immediately delivering two fluttering, whimpering downward runs that disarmed one, and that dissolved into squeaks, freshly coined notes, and rhythmic displacements. (It is hard to think of a jazz musician who has exhibited more naked emotion than Coleman.) Dolphy, a young West Coast musician and one of Coleman's first apostles, chimed in with his bass clarinet, producing a tone that alternated between moos and a hubble-bubble, and for several measures the two jostled each other, dissonantly and marvelously, providing a singular example of dual improvisation. The brief second section, which displayed some tempoless impressionistic spinach that was rudely swept aside by a yawp from Coleman, gave way to a medium-tempo sequence in which LaFaro, an extraordinary bassist, and Dolphy, on bass clarinet again, played a double cadenza set off by the strings. The textural contrasts alone were memorable—high, rapid, spin-sterish notes from the bass, the deep-blue-sea sounds of Dolphy in his lowest register, and the background breezes of the quartet. The last section was a kind of decompression period. Then came "Conversations," in which written and improvised sections succeed each other. This rendition, which included a remarkable solo by Bill Evans, was followed by the most striking effort of the evening—the atonal "Abstraction No. 1," written recently for Coleman. The composition, one of those rare artless pieces that seem to fashion themselves right on the spot, had a resiliency that was the result of the written and improvised interplay between the string quartet and Coleman. The strings first struck off follow-the-leader chips of sound that appeared to have been extracted from old Coleman solos. Coleman jousted appreciatively with the strings, joined them briefly, and abruptly sailed into a bucking solo that was underlined by the strings with an ecstasy of pushing, chanting sounds. Then Coleman sedately re-entered the ensemble for a further exchange of compliments, and the piece ended. Composition and improvisation had been organically and inextricably linked.

After the intermission, the number was refreshingly performed again, complete with a new segment of the Coleman canon, and next there was an impressive tour de force, "Transformation," which was originally unveiled a few years back. Here a "classical" passage is gradually coupled with a regular beat, diminishes, and is supplanted by an improvised section, which in this performance was played by Evans. A ground swell, in the form of a riff, appears, and then two parts—written and improvised—pump away neck and neck to the finish line. A new work, "Variants on a Theme of John Lewis," followed, and it had much of the coherence of "Abstraction No. 1." Based on Lewis's lovely "Django"—a tribute to Django Reinhardt—it began with Galbraith, who played the melody in a sorrowing, bareheaded fashion. The rhythm section and the vibraphone entered; LaFaro soloed and then joined forces with Galbraith; Dolphy, on flute, and LaFaro collaborated handsomely; the quartet slipped in some Reinhardt tremolos; and the piece slowly assumed a glistening, spidery air. The closing section trailed off, pressing the last drops from Lewis's melody. The finale was another fresh composition, "Progression in Tempo," a blues done as a rhythmic experiment, in which the tempo was gradually speeded up and then abruptly doubled. Fortunately, the number was anticlimactic, allowing one to settle peacefully back to earth.

This concert engraved on my mind, I had dinner with Coleman soon after at a restaurant on West Eleventh Street. He arrived carrying an instrument case, a navel orange, and a tightly furled umbrella, which swung easily from his left arm. A handsome man of medium height, dressed in an impeccable dark-green suit and a black-tie, and wearing a beard, Coleman checked his case and umbrella, placed the orange carefully beside his butter plate, shook hands in a self-deprecating way, sat down and, without hesitation, began a concentrated, nonstop monologue that had a lot in common with one of his solos: "I'm not very hungry. I just ate a little while ago, but I'll have a small Salisbury steak and a salad, maybe with some Thousand Island dressing. I haven't heard one person yet who can explain what I'm doing. People laugh at me, shake their heads. But I won't let any of that affect me. There's but one thing you can do —play the true essence of yourself. Talent and appearances have nothing to do with each other. Look at Van Gogh. He cut off his ear; it didn't hurt his talent. Most people fail to hear what is being played at the *moment* it is played. They pay more attention to behavior and what they see than to what is happening musically. I know exactly what I'm doing. I'm beginning where Charlie Parker stopped. Parker's melodic lines were placed across ordinary chord progressions. My melodic approach is based on phrasing, and my phrasing is an extension of how I hear the intervals and pitch of the tunes I play. There is no end to pitch. You can play flat in tune and sharp in tune. It's a question of vibration. My phrasing is spontaneous, not a style. A style happens when your phrasing hardens. Jazz music is the only music in which the same note can be played night after night but differently each time. It's the hidden things, the subconscious that lies in the body and lets you know: you feel this, you play this. Do you understand that? After all, *music* is harmless. It all depends on which way a person is using it. I give my musicians one of my tunes and tell them, 'You play that your way. You add to it what you can. Enlarge it. Extend it.' But this isn't easy, I know. The other night, at a rehearsal for the concert I played in of Gunther Schuller's music, Schuller made me play a little four-measure thing he'd written six or seven times before I got it right. I could read it, see the notes on the paper. But I heard those notes in my head, heard their pitch, and what I heard was different from what Schuller heard. Then I got it right. I got it his way. It was as simple as that."

Coleman paused abruptly, picked up the orange, hefted it, and rolled it around reflectively in his hands. I asked him to tell me about his early career. "I started playing the alto when I was about fourteen," he said, replacing the orange and attacking his Salisbury steak. "My family couldn't afford to give me lessons, so I bought an instruction book and taught myself, but I taught myself wrong. I thought the low C on my horn was the A in the book, and when I joined a church band the leader said, 'Look at this boy. Playing the instrument wrong for two years. He'll never be a saxophone player.' You can't live down your mistakes, but if you keep thinking about them you can't emerge from them, either. I hooked up with a carnival band, then a rhythm-and-blues group, which stranded me in California in 1950. They kept telling me in that band I was doing this wrong, doing that wrong. In the next six, seven years, I traveled back and forth between Fort Worth and California, playing once in a while but doing day work mostly —stockboy, houseboy, freight-elevator operator. By 1957, I had got very depressed in California, and I wired my ma would she send me a bus ticket home, and on the day the ticket arrived, Les Koenig, of Contemporary Records, asked me to audition some of my tunes for him. I did, and he gave me my first record session. I began playing around California, and in 1959 John Lewis heard me in Frisco and asked me to come to the School of Jazz, at Lenox, Massachusetts, that summer, and after that, since I felt I'd never got a chance to exist properly, to know what I truly am, I migrated to New York. Now I'm set. Or, anyway, set to be set.

What I'd like most now is a vacation, but I've got three musicians depending on me. I'm tired. Six hours a night, six nights a week. Sometimes I go to the club and I can't understand what I feel. 'Am I here? How will I make it through tonight?' I say to myself. I'd like to play a couple of nights a week is all. I'd have more to say. I'd get closer to harnessing my feelings, to getting down to the true essence. Well, it's time to work."

Coleman yawned, picked up his orange, and tossed it into the air.

"What are you going to do with that orange?" I asked.

"Why, eat it, man," he said, laughing. "What else? An orange is very pleasant one, two o'clock in the morning."

Mingus

UNTIL 1939, when Jimmy Blanton appeared, the bass fiddle had occupied the position in jazz of a reliable tackle. It had, a decade before, replaced the tuba in the rhythm section, and its best practitioners—Pops Foster, Al Morgan, Wellman Braud, Milt Hinton, Walter Page, and John Kirby—had become adept at rigid timekeeping and at itemizing the chords of each tune. These bassists also boasted tones that could be felt and even heard in the biggest groups. But they rarely soloed, and, when they did, restricted themselves to on-the-beat statements that were mostly extensions of their ensemble playing. Blanton, who died in 1942, at the age of twenty-one, abruptly changed all this by converting the bass into a hornlike instrument that could be used both rhythmically and melodically. Since then, the bass has taken over the rhythmic burdens once carried by the pianist's left hand and by the bass drum, and it has added a new melodic voice to the ensemble. At the same time, a group of Blanton-inspired bassists have sprung up to meet these new duties, and have included such remarkable performers as Oscar Pettiford, Ray Brown, Red Mitchell, Wilbur Ware, Paul Chambers, Scott LaFaro, and Charlie Mingus. All are first-rate accompanists and soloists, and all possess exceptional techniques. The youngest have even begun to wander toward the fenceless meadows of atonality. Chief among these bassists is Mingus, the greatest pizzicato player the instrument has had. He is also the first modern jazz musician who has successfully combined virtuosity, the revolutions brought about by Charlie Parker, and the lyricism of such pre-bebop performers as Ben Webster, the boogie-woogie pianists, and Billie Holiday.

Like many contemporary jazz musicians, Mingus is far more than an instrumentalist. He is a formidable composer-arranger and a beneficent martinet who invariably finds, hires, and trains talented but unknown men. A big, loosely packed man of thirty-eight, with a handsome face and wary, intelligent eyes, Mingus is an indefatigable iconoclast. He is a member of no movement and vociferously abhors musical cant. He denounces rude audiences to their faces. (A recent scolding, administered in a New York night club, was tape-recorded on the spot, and has been printed in an anthology of jazz pieces. It is a heartening piece of hortatory Americana.) He unabashedly points out his colleagues' shams and weaknesses in his album-liner notes or in crackling letters to magazines like *Down Beat*. When tongue and pen fail him, he uses his fists. Mingus compresses all this dedication into his playing, which is daring, furious, and precise. Despite the blurred tonal properties of the bass, Mingus forces a kaleidoscope of sounds from it. However, much of the time he uses a penetrating tone that recalls such men as Foster and Braud, and that is especially effective in his accompanying, where it shines through the loudest collective passages. (It sometimes shines so brightly that Mingus, in the manner of Sidney Bechet, unintentionally becomes the lead instrument.) Mingus's supporting work is an indissoluble mixture of the rhythmic and the melodic. By seemingly playing hob with the beat—restlessly pulling it forward with double-time inserts, rapid tremolos, or staccato patterns, reining it in with whoa-babe legato figures, or jumping stoutly up and down on it—he achieves the rhythmic locomotion of drummers like Sid Catlett and Jo Jones. Yet he carefully fits these devices to each soloist, lying low when a musician is carrying his own weight, and coming forward brusquely and cheerfully to aid the lame and the halt. It is almost impossible to absorb all of Mingus at a single hearing. In addition to carrying out his rhythmic tasks, he simultaneously constructs attractive and frequently beautiful melodic lines. These may shadow a soloist, or they may be fashioned into counterlines that either plump the soloist up or accidentally upstage him. Mingus is a dangerous man to play with.

He is also an exhilarating soloist. Because he is the sort of virtuoso who has long since transcended his instrument, his finest solos are an eloquent, seemingly disembodied *music*. The pizzicato bass was not designed for the timbres Mingus extracts from it. He may hit a note as if it were a piece of wood, getting a clipped thup. He may make a note reverberate or, rubbing his left hand quickly down the finger board, turn it into an abrasive glissando. Sometimes he fingers with the nails of his left hand, achieving a rattling sound. Or he may uncoop a string of whispered notes that barely stir the air. He will start a solo in a medium-tempo blues with a staccato, deck-clearing phrase, cut his volume in half, play an appealing blues melody that suggests the 1928 Louis Armstrong, step up his volume, line out a complex, whirring phrase that may climb and fall with a cicadalike insistency for a couple of measures, develop another plaintive a-b-c figure, improvise on it rhythmically, insert a couple of sweeping smears, and go into an arpeggio that may cover several octaves and that, along the way, will be decorated with unexpected accents. Mingus's solos in ballad numbers are equally majestic. He often plays the first chorus almost straight, hovering behind, over, and in front of the melody—italicizing a note here, adding a few notes there, falling silent now and then to let a figure expand—and finishing up with an embossed now-listen-to-this air. There are only half a dozen jazz soloists skilled enough for such complacency.

Mingus the bassist is indivisible from Mingus the leader. He conducts with his bass, setting the tempos and emotional level of each tune with his introductory phrases, toning the ensemble up or down with his volume or simply with sharp stares, and injecting his soloists with countless c.c.s of his own energy. His methods of composition are equally dictatorial and are a fascinating variation of Duke Ellington's. Mingus has explained them in a liner note:

My present working methods use very little written material. I "write" compositions on mental score paper, then I lay out the composition part by part to the musicians. I play them the "framework" on piano so that they are all familiar with my interpretation and feeling and with the scale and chord progressions. . . . Each man's particular style is taken into consideration. They are given different rows of notes to use against each chord but they choose their own notes and play them in their own style, from scales as well as chords, except where a particular mood is indicated. In this way I can keep my own compositional flavor . . . and yet allow the musicians more individual freedom in the creation of their group lines and solos.

Most of his recent work can be divided into three parts—the eccentric, the lyrical, and the hot. His eccentric efforts have included experiments with poetry and prose readings and attempts to fold non-musical sounds (whistles, ferryboats docking, foghorns, and the like) into his instrumental timbres. The results have been amusing but uneasy; one tends to automatically weed out the extracurricular effects in order to get at the underlying music. The lyrical Mingus is a different matter. His best ballad-type melodies are constructed in wide, curving lines that form small, complete études rather than mere tunes. Their content dictates their form, which resembles the ragtime structures of Jelly Roll Morton or the miniature concertos of Duke Ellington, both of whom Mingus has learned from. But Mingus has been most successful with the blues and with gospel or church-type music. The pretensions that becloud some of his other efforts lift, leaving intense, single-minded pieces. More important than the use of different tempos and rhythms in these compositions, which repeatedly pick the music up and put it down, are their contrapuntal, semi-improvised ensembles, in which each instrument loosely follows a melodic line previously sketched out by Mingus. The results are raucous and unplaned, and they raise a brave flag for a new and genuine collective improvisation.

Mingus's most recent records—"Mingus Ah Um" (Columbia), "Blues & Roots" (Atlantic), and "Mingus Dynasty" (Columbia)—offer some spectacular things. Most of the compositions are by Mingus and are played by nine- or ten-piece groups (a size beyond the budgets of most of the offbeat night clubs in which Mingus generally performs), which employ his collective techniques with considerable aplomb, thus pointing a way out of the box that the big band built itself into before its decline. Mingus delivers a fireside chat on the problem in the notes to the second Columbia record:

> The same big bands with four or five trumpets, four or five trombones, five or six saxophones, and a rhythm section . . . still [play] arrangements as though there were only three instruments in the band: a trumpet, a trombone, and a saxophone, with the other . . . trumpets . . . trombones . . . and saxophones there just to make the arrangement sound louder by playing harmonic support. . . . What would you call this? A big band? A loud band? A jazz band? A creative band?
>
> I'd write for a big sound (and with fewer musicians) by thinking out the form that each instrument *as an individual* is going to play in

relation to *all* the others in the composition. This would replace the old-hat system of passing the melody from section to section . . . while the trombones run through their routine of French horn chordal sounds. . . . I think it's time to discard these tired arrangements and save only the big Hollywood production introduction and ending which uses a ten or more note chord. If these ten notes were used as a starting point for several melodies and finished as a linear composition—with parallel or simultaneous juxtaposed melodic thoughts—we might come up with some creative big-band jazz.

The Atlantic record provides several first-rate demonstrations of this approach. On hand with Mingus are Jackie McLean and John Handy, alto saxophones; Booker Ervin, tenor saxophone; Pepper Adams, baritone saxophone; Jimmy Knepper and Willie Dennis, trombones; Horace Parlan or Mal Waldron, piano; and Dannie Richmond, drums. There are six numbers, all blues by Mingus. One of the best is the fast "E's Flat Ah's Flat Too." The baritone saxophone opens by itself with a choppy *ostinato* figure, and is joined, in madrigal fashion, by the trombones, which deliver a graceful, slightly out-of-harmony riff. The drums, bass, and piano slide into view. The trombones pursue a new melody, the baritone continues its subterranean figure, and the tenor saxophone enters, carrying still another line. Several choruses have elapsed. Then one of the alto saxophones slowly climbs into a solo above the entire ensemble, which, with all its voices spinning, becomes even more intense when Mingus starts shouting at the top of his voice, like a growl trumpet. Solos follow, giving way to the closing ensemble, which pumps off into twelve straight choruses of rough, continually evolving improvisations on the shorter opening ensemble. Near the end, Mingus starts bellowing again, and then everything abruptly grows sotto-voce. The trombones dip into a brief melodic aside, and the piece closes in a maelstrom, with each instrument heading in a different direction. New tissues of sound emerge in this number and all the others at each hearing—a shift in tempo, a subtle theme being carried far in the background by a saxophone, a riff by the trombones that is a minor variation on one used in the preceding chorus.

The Columbia records, which include eighteen numbers (all but two by Mingus) and pretty much the same personnel, are not as headlong. "Mingus Ah Um" has a couple of ballads, more blues, and, most important, generous amounts of the satire that is present in almost everything Mingus writes. This quality is most noticeable in "Fables of Faubus," which concentrates on two themes—an appealing and rather melancholy lament, and a sarcastic, smeared figure, played by the trombones in a pompous, puppetlike rhythm. At one point, the two melodies—one bent-backed, the other swaggering—are played side by side; the effect is singular. Mingus's needling is more subdued in pieces on Lester Young ("Goodbye Pork Pie Hat"), Ellington ("Open Letter to Duke"), and Charlie Parker ("Bird Calls"). But it emerges again in a delightful twitting of Jelly Roll Morton, called "Jelly Roll," which manages to suggest both the lumbering aspects of Morton's piano *and* his gift for handsome melodies. "Mingus Dynasty" has pleasant, reverent reworkings of a couple of Ellington numbers; a somewhat attenuated selection called "Far Wells,

Mill Valley," written in three sections for piano, vibraphone, flute, four saxophones, trumpet, trombone, bass, and drums; and a fresh version of one of Mingus's gospel numbers, "Wednesday Night Prayer Meeting," this one called "Slop."

Mingus has never had a substantial following, and it is easy to see why: he courts only himself and his own genius. A one-man clique, he invents his own fashions and discards them when they are discovered by others. The content of his compositions is often repellent; it can be ornery, sarcastic, and bad-tempered. His own overbearing, high-tension playing pinions its listeners, often demanding more than they can give. In happier days, Mingus's music might have caused riots.

The Ragtime Game

RAGTIME IS by no means dead and gone. Indeed, it flickers bravely on, and the principal keeper of the flame is Joseph F. Lamb, who, at seventy-two, is the last of the big three among ragtime composers, the other two being Scott Joplin (1868-1917) and James Scott (1886-1938). Lamb first slid into my vision when I received an L.P. from Folkways Records titled "Joseph Lamb: A Study in Classic Ragtime," a collection of ten Lamb rags, played by him and recorded last summer at his home, in Brooklyn. After I had listened to the record, which is the first Lamb has ever made, I phoned him to ask if I could pay him a visit. "Be delighted!" he shouted over the telephone. "I'm a little hard of hearing, if that doesn't bother you. Take the B.-M.T. Brighton local and get off at Avenue U. I'm five short blocks away. Any time after two."

Before boarding the Brighton Beach local, I did some homework on Lamb, and discovered that his reputation rests on just twelve rags, published between 1908 and 1919; that he has as many or more unpublished rags, some of them written in the last couple of years; that he had known Scott Joplin; and that he was rediscovered by Rudi Blesh in 1950, when Blesh, who was doing research for a book called *They All Played Ragtime*, found that "Joseph Lamb" was not, as had long been believed, a pseudonym of Scott Joplin's but that Joseph Lamb was a once celebrated contemporary of Joplin's and was still very much alive. Thus equipped, I arrived at a little past two at Lamb's house, a small brown shingled one not far from Coney Island.

I was greeted by both Lamb, a slight, jovial, big-voiced, bespectacled, gray-haired man with a thin face and a long, generous nose, and Mrs. Lamb, a short, pretty woman, and they ushered me into a small front room furnished with two television sets, three bamboo chairs, and a mahogany secretary. When I was seated, I asked Lamb if he had had much response to his record. "Well, it's pretty hard to fathom!" he boomed. "I've got letters from all over, and Rudi Blesh called up immediately after he'd heard the record, and said, 'It's wonderful, Joe, wonderful.' It's no fault of mine that I'm still alive, and I guess the fact I am means a lot to these people. I'm not a conceited man, but I can't say I'm not pleased about it. It's got me playing once more, even though I don't catch everything I play, because of my hearing. Since Blesh's book, I've started writing rags again, which isn't easy, either. I can hear in my head what I want to put on paper, but I can't tell if it sounds right on the piano. That record was a hell of an experience. I was all out of practice and didn't much want to do it, but Sam Charters, who made it, pestered me and pestered me, and finally he came out here on a hot day and we did it. Who ever knew that stuff was going to come back?" Lamb shook his head in bewilderment, and Mrs. Lamb, who had slipped out of the room, returned and set down a glass of apricot juice and a plate of Lorna Doones next to him.

"Something to wet your whistle!" she shouted at him.

"Well, good," Lamb said, and took a sip. "I was born in Montclair, New Jersey, and taught myself the piano. My sisters used to tell each other 'That Joe will be a composer. You watch.' Pretty soon I was writing two-steps, waltzes, and intermezzos—the 'Florentine Waltz,' 'I Love You Just the Same,' and 'My Fairy Iceberg Queen,' which started out as a cowboy song. In 1904, after I'd graduated from St. Jerome's College, near Toronto, I went to work in New York in a wholesale-dry-goods place, and I was buying a lot of sheet music. Gimbel's and Macy's used to have seven- and eight-cent sales on it Saturdays. I found I was partial to rags, particularly the harder kind, and then Scott Joplin's 'Maple Leaf Rag' hit me good and proper. Ninety-five per cent of the best rags were written by Negroes, you know, and I seemed to fall right in with their things. In 1907, I wrote my first rag, the 'Sensation Rag.' One day around then, I was in the office of John Stark, the music publisher, where I bought most of my rags. There was a colored man sitting in a corner, his foot gouty and wrapped up, and crutches beside him. I was telling Mrs. Stark how much I admired Scott Joplin and how I'd like to meet him, and she said, 'Is that so? Well, here's your man,' and pointed to the colored fellow. I don't know what I said, I was so worked up. He was my pattern in the ragtime game. We left together, and he said did I mind if he walked along with me? I was tickled to death, you can imagine. Later, I went up to his boarding house, in Harlem, and played 'Sensation' for him, and he suggested a few changes. I had a chromatic scale going up the keyboard in both hands in one place, and he said, 'Make that left-hand scale go down instead of up.' He persuaded Stark to publish 'Sensation,' and Stark gave me twenty-five dollars for it, and twenty-five more after the first thousand copies were sold. After that, Stark published the 'Excelsior Rag,' the 'Ethiopia Rag,' the 'American Beauty Rag,' and all the rest. I stopped writing rags around 1920, when ragtime went out. The stimulation was gone. I've never made any money from my rags. The satisfaction of getting them published and on the counters is what mattered to me, and still matters. I've got seventeen rags right here, unpublished, some of them fifty years old."

"If you sell them all, you'll be a millionaire, Joe," Mrs. Lamb said, and laughed.

" 'Bird-Brain Rag' is one of them," Lamb said. "Nobody likes the title. What's the matter with them? The first strain starts like a bird. Listen."

Lamb hopped up, disappeared into his living room, sat down at an upright, and played a quick five-note bird phrase.

"That doesn't sound like a bird, it sounds like a bugle call, Joe," Mrs. Lamb said, and laughed again.

Lamb returned to his chair, puffing a little, and said, "I've got all the time I need now. I retired in 1957, after forty-four years with a factoring concern

in the import-export line. Who knows about ragtime? A fellow was here from N.B.C. last week and
said they might do a ragtime program in the fall,
and Burl Ives is helping me join A.S.C.A.P. I'm
writing rags again after forty years. I get these seventeen published, I'll do seventeen more."

David and Goliath

It is not common knowledge that *two* jazz festivals
were held in Newport over the Fourth of July
weekend—the multi-engined Newport Festival (sev-
enth model) and a far smaller wind-driven affair,
Jazz at Cliff Walk Manor. Nor is it generally known
that when the dust from the crash of the big festival, which was abruptly closed on Sunday afternoon,
had subsided, the rump festival was still going
strong. Suffice it to say that the riot that destroyed
the Newport Festival was the work of amusical yahoos of college age, many of them barefoot, loutish,
overvitamined, and, in the case of men, effeminately
dressed in pedal-pushers. No one involved was badly
damaged, which is miraculous when one considers
this item from a long and superbly detailed story in
next morning's Providence *Sunday Journal*: "State
Police Cpl. Peter J. O'Connell was giving orders to
half a dozen uniformed state police when he suddenly fell unconscious, struck on the nose by a flying
full beer can. He later regained consciousness and
appeared not seriously hurt." Moreover, the outcome
of the unofficial contest between the two festivals
produced an unavoidable state of irony. The Cliff
Walk Manor festival, hastily organized a couple of

weeks before by Charlie Mingus and Max Roach, constituted a rebellion against what they claimed was the small pay the Newport Festival accorded its lesser-known attractions, as well as against its mastodon ways. That the two enterprises should suddenly find themselves serving as David and Goliath was melodrama of a high order.

The Cliff Walk Manor festival was held on the football-field-size lawn of the Cliff Walk Manor Hotel, a stucco-and-red-brick mansion high above Easton's Beach and just three or four city blocks east of Freebody Park, the site of the other festival, which, as long as it lasted, overlaid this one with a steady flow of sounds. The C.W.M. festival was virtually handmade by the musicians involved, who constructed a bandstand, decorated it in a fire-engine red, enclosed the lawn with snow fencing, erected half a dozen tents to sleep in, procured five hundred undertakers' chairs, issued handbills, and, after the weekend was in progress, collected contributions from onlookers outside of the fence. The lawn sloped accommodatingly toward the bandstand, where the musicians, silhouetted against distant Middletown, resembled figures in a vast diorama. Gulls, swallows, and an occasional helicopter circled their heads, and the shumm-shumm-shumm of the waves below provided—especially during bass solos—a majestic background. When it rained, as it did on Friday and Sunday nights, the proceedings were moved into a square, airy room in the hotel. (By Sunday night, Freebody Park stood empty and silent, and the wrangling thunderstorm that took place had an unnerving Jehovah air.)

The C.W.M. festival had its own private ironies. Free to play as they wished, the musicians involved —on hand all weekend, along with various ringers, were the Max Roach quintet, the Charlie Mingus Jazz Workshop, the Ornette Coleman quartet, the Coleman Hawkins-Jo Jones quartet, and a six-piece pickup outfit led by Kenny Dorham—performed mainly as if the assembly-line procedures of the Newport Festival, at which most of them had appeared at one time or another, had been stamped into their spirits. Sets were often limited to three or four numbers, the concerts (afternoons excepted) were too long, and the same tunes were offered over and over again. Roach's quintet played a slow, lengthy, bagpipe dirge, built chiefly around his drumming, no less than four times. The first hearing was delightful; the second was absorbing for the improvisational contrasts it afforded; the third was abrasive; and the fourth was torture. But there were corrective moments. These came when personnels were temporarily shuffled or pared down for such things as a duet by Mingus and Roach; a lengthy free improvisation by Mingus, Roach, Coleman, and Dorham; a collaboration by Dorham, Hawkins, and Jones; and a couple of Near Eastern love songs performed by Ahmed Abdul-Malik, the Roach bassist, on the oud, a large Egyptian stringed instrument that resembles a gourd sliced in half.

Four notable things occurred during the opening concert, on Thursday evening. Wilbur Ware, the bassist in Dorham's group (Allen Eager on alto saxophone, Teddy Charles, Kenny Drew, and Arthur Taylor), fashioned a solo in "Lover Man" that was a masterpiece. Ware stands alone among modern bass players. His work is not patterned on that of Jimmy Blanton, but is restricted to an on-the-beat attack and singsong harmonic investigations that give the impression of someone striding purposefully over uneven ground. Later, Coleman Hawkins, accompanied by Drew, Ware, and Jones, played half a dozen choruses in "Lover Come Back to Me" (fast) and "September Song" (slow), which insinuated their way into one's marrow. In the fast number, Jones took a long solo with his hands, scraping the drumheads, snapping them disdainfully with his fingernails, and cleaving them with the edges of his palms. Baby Laurence did two numbers, backed by Mingus's group, that, with the help of a couple of microphones tilted against the front edge of the platform on which he danced, went off like machine guns.

The next afternoon was parceled among reshuffled groups, which huddled beneath two enormous yellow-and-green beach umbrellas when it began drizzling. The evening performance, which had more first-rate Hawkins and Ware, as well as a nearly vicious rendition by the Mingus group (Booker Ervin, Eric Dolphy, Ted Curson, and Danny Richmond) of a Mingus gospel number, "Better Git It in Your Soul," dissolved into a jam session that continued until four in the morning. (The C.W.M.'s only yahoos arrived around three, and, half a dozen strong, stood beerily about for ten minutes or so, bare feet matting the floor, peacock-colored shirts hanging out, pedal-pushers tight and wrinkled.) Abdul-Malik conversed with his oud, Roach performed a ten-minute drum solo, and Mingus and Roach engaged in a duet. This was followed by a free-for-all by Mingus, Roach, Dorham, Julian Priester (Roach's trombonist), and Coleman. It provoked Mingus into one of the best solos he has ever played, while Roach softly tapped his drumsticks together in the background. The same group, minus Priester, appeared the next afternoon, and, taking advantage of the preliminaries of the previous night, developed a totally free improvisation that lasted for nearly three-quarters of an hour. Each man soloed several times, tempos rose and fell, sea-swell interludes came and went, and the piece was closed by a long, zigzagging collective atonal ensemble. The Saturday-evening concert was embellished by the presence of Roy Eldridge, who worked with the Hawkins-Jones group, and by Ornette Coleman, who when all was said and done, emerged as the champion of the weekend. All the twenty or so numbers performed during the festival by Coleman's band, which included Don Cherry, Charlie Haden and Eddie Blackwell (drums), were by the leader and all were different. Coleman reached his peak on Saturday night in a new and lovely medium-slow number. His solo, free of the commotion he often raises in his relentless search for unknown sounds, had an affecting directness and simplicity.

The Thursday concert at Cliff Walk Manor had an attendance of ten. By Sunday hundreds were on hand. Throughout there was a catching bonhomie between all present, and this, together with Roach's emceeing, gave the event an unfailing smoothness and graciousness. Best of all, there wasn't an impresario in sight; they were, of course, just up the street.

Walpurgis Night

It is no longer fashionable or even polite to suggest that many Negro jazz musicians possess certain built-in gifts—a sense of rhythm, physical dexterity and grace, an aptitude for great improvisation—that are rarely granted their white colleagues. Indeed, to propose that Negro musicians are blessed with such characteristics has become a reverse heresy. Scientists, doing a variation on Lysenko, snort at the theory, while many jazz critics regard it as an admission of counteracting and less pleasant characteristics. Be that as it may, those misguided jazz admirers who are sufficiently brave to cross picket lines to give Negro jazz musicians their due have, if nothing else, irrefutable statistics on their side. Thus, there have been dozens of first-rate Negro musicians and, give or take a Gerry Mulligan or Stan Getz, only five comparable white musicians: Bix Beiderbecke, Dave Tough, Pee Wee Russell, Jack Teagarden, and Django Reinhardt. There have, however, been plenty of white jazz musicians who, lacking this or that elusive quality, have been almost men instead of merely highly talented boys. One of these is Buddy Rich, who remains the greatest virtuoso in jazz drumming.

A lithe, compact, nervous, temperamental man with close-cropped hair and a gladiator handsomeness, Rich has had an explosive history that began on the vaudeville stage when he was eighteen months old and that has carried him through the bands of Bunny Berigan, Artie Shaw, Tommy Dorsey, Count Basie, and Harry James, through Norman Granz's "Jazz at the Philharmonic," through recording sessions with everyone from Art Tatum to Charlie Parker, and through innumerable groups of his own. Rich came into prominence in the early forties with Dorsey, ran neck and neck for several years with his principal model, Gene Krupa, eclipsed him, and in turn was eclipsed by the tumultuous arrival of bebop and the new school of jazz drumming led by Max Roach. Nonetheless, Rich's influence, which has been considerable, is still visible. Among others, Louis Bellson, Ed Shaughnessy, and Shelly Manne have admired him, and so have latecomers like Joe Morello, Philly Joe Jones, and Frank Butler. Almost none of them, however, have matched his technical prowess (Bellson is the only exception).

Aside from his debt to Krupa, Rich's style is his own. It appears at first to be just about flawless. Monolithic and commanding, Rich has an infallible beat, and the exuberance to make that beat catching. His playing is clean and decisive, and he never misses a stroke. He is a proficient ensemble man and a frequently stunning soloist. But those qualities are not enough—or, rather, they are too much. Overpowered by his astonishing gifts, Rich has become a captive of his own virtuosity. As a result, the felicities that have made less well-equipped drummers, such as Sid Catlett and Jo Jones, his superiors have been almost completely crowded out. He has little sense of taste, dynamics, and shading, and none of the elasticity essential to great drumming. His playing never changes, his solos are often militaristic and far too long, and in general he projects an uncompromising rigidity that tends to flatten rather than elevate his cohorts.

For all of Rich's energy and steadiness, he is a peculiarly dull accompanist. One reason lies in the way he tunes his drums. They give off a dry, stale sound that never blends tonally with the other instruments. Another reason is plain unimaginativeness. Instead of sympathetic timbres behind a soloist (the ocean motion of Jo Jones's high-hat cymbals, Catlett's rimshots, the sleigh-bell tintinnabulations of Connie Kay's ride-cymbal figures), one is conscious only of a metronomic deliberation. His cymbal work is light and clear, but it evaporates before it has taken effect, while his accents on the bass drum and snare are limited to thuds and implacable rimshots, fired exactly where expected. All of Rich's accompanying has, in sum, a now-is-it-my-turn-yet? air. When his turn does come, his face exhibits agony, his body contracts, taking on a ball shape, his arms blur, his drumsticks break and rocket about. For many years, there was no selectivity in Rich's solos, no chance for the listener to sort out what was happening. Recently, though, he has begun to construct them instead of merely spawning them. His best ones occur in middle tempos. He may begin on his snare with a series of I.B.M. beats arranged intensely on or near the beat (from which he never wanders far), insert cracked-knuckle rimshots and short rolls, drop Big Ben offbeats on the bass drum, intensify his snare-and-rimshot patterns, and, bringing his auxiliary arms into action, overlay these patterns with staccato cymbal strokes. Gradually, this duplex figure grows increasingly solid as he forces more and more beats into spaces seemingly already filled. By this time, his virtuosity has begun to devour him. Casting aside all that has come before, he rotates, crisscrosses, and trampolins around his set, moving with incredible speed from snare to tom-tom to cymbals to snare to cymbals to tom-tom snare cymbals cymbals snare tom-tomsnaretomtomtom. . . . Walpurgis Night. High winds. Thunder and lightning. And even though what he is playing has ceased to make any musical sense, it has become the sort of high-wire exhibitionism that compels the listener to jump up and make foolish sounds. Then, a hypercrescendo is reached, and suddenly it is over. The roar drifts smartly away, the ball unfurls, the arms slip back into focus, the face smiles, and the ovation—a kind of coda to the solo itself—begins.

All that need be known about Rich can be found on two records, "Buddy and Sweets" (Verve) and "Rich versus Roach" (Mercury). "Buddy and Sweets," made with Harry Edison, Jimmy Rowles, and John Simmons, contains two of the best and most conservative solos Rich has recorded. (There are seven numbers in all.) These occur in "Yellow Rose of Brooklyn," which is taken at a very fast tempo, and in the medium "Barney's Bugle." In the second solo, which Rich holds down to five minutes, he pauses now and then before falling into his customary trance, and there are even a few round-the-set explosions, topped with silence, that suggest the timing of Catlett—a comparison that might not please Rich. Here is the pianist Billy Taylor reminiscing, in a book called *Hear Me Talkin' to Ya*, about Rich versus Catlett: "Sid was a great soloist and a great showman. He was completely at home musically in whatever he was doing. I remember once on the Coast, when Buddy Rich, Dodo Marmarosa, and Buddy De Franco were all with Tommy Dorsey, they used to come into the clubs and cut everybody. [Rich] was cutting all the drummers, but not Sid. It used to annoy Buddy so much. He'd play all over his head—play fantastically—and then Sid would gently get back on the stand, and play his simple, melodic lines—on drums—and he'd make his point."

The Mercury record is rewarding for the way in which Rich's rigidity and Roach's limpidity offset each other. There are eight numbers, in which two small groups led by Rich and Roach collaborate, giving way frequently for short exchanges and full-length excursions between the drummers. Rich comes through best in the medium "Sing, Sing, Sing (With a Swing)," where he is in a nervous rim-shot mood, and in the slower "Big Foot," a blues in which he matches double-time breaks with Roach. "Figure Eights" consists of four and one half minutes of Rich and Roach trading breaks at a tempo faster than the ordinary mortal can tap his foot to. The inevitable happens. After Rich's third break, a sensational bit of broken-field running, the two men attempt to quell one another by falling into a series of buzzes—Rich: zzzzzzzzzzz; Roach: zzZ-zzZZZzzZ; Rich: ZZZZZZZzzZZ, and so forth. But there has been no contest; a sundial doesn't stand a chance with a clock.

Part Three: 1961

The Rabbit Returns

THE CELEBRATED FICKLENESS indulged in by admirers of the arts, most of whom resemble housewives selecting cantaloupes, reaches epic proportions among jazz audiences. Thus, the Original Dixieland Jazz Band, flourishing in 1920, had been largely forgotten by 1930. In 1935, King Oliver, famous less than a decade earlier, was in total obscurity. The *nouvelle vague* of Charlie Parker, Dizzy Gillespie, and Stan Kenton had, by the late forties, replaced almost completely such recent landmarks as Count Basie, Benny Goodman, Ben Webster, Art Tatum, and even Duke Ellington. This capriciousness increased in the fifties. Gillespie was abruptly set aside for Miles Davis. Basie reappeared and Kenton went under. Woody Herman, pumping furiously in the forties, became largely a memory, while a West Coast movement made up of musicians like Shorty Rogers, Shelly Manne, and Jimmy Giuffre rose and fell precipitously. Sonny Rollins burst briefly into view, then was overtaken by John Coltrane, and early in 1960 Ornette Coleman blanked everyone out. The reasons for these lightning love-hate cycles are fairly clear. Jazz thrives both artistically and socially on rebellion; indeed, it is the most liberal of musics. Until recently, its audiences have been composed mainly of the young, who relish such hot sauces. And these audiences, more unskilled than not, often train their ears only on what they are told is worthy by the jazz press, which tends to confuse newness with progress and progress with quality. One of the most striking victims of this fickleness has been the fifty-four-year-old alto saxophonist Johnny Hodges. Unlike many other swing musicians, Hodges was toppled by a double whammy. He suffered, along with his colleagues, from the rise of bebop, but he also suffered because the leader of that movement, Charlie Parker, played the same instrument. When Parker died, in 1955, Hodges had become an out-of-fashion leader of a small semi-rock-and-roll group. However, the tastemakers were at work, and by 1959 Parker's enormous ghost had been sufficiently laid to allow Hodges to win the *Down Beat* critics' poll, an award that paid a considerable compliment to Hodges' staying powers and none at all to the fitful perceptions of those who had voted it.

A short, taciturn man with a beak nose, heavily lidded eyes, and an impassive Oriental air, Hodges, who is incongruously known as Rabbit, has been almost perpetually bound up with Duke Ellington since 1928. (He left the Ellington band in 1951 but rejoined it, apparently for good, in 1955.) Unlike most Ellington musicians, who have unwittingly come to depend on Ellington for balance and inspiration and who generally head downward when they leave the band, Hodges functions well with and without Ellington. He is most comfortable in a small band, which became plain in the late thirties and early forties on those invaluable records made by chamber groups from the Ellington band. Nearly nonpareil among Ellingtonians, Hodges has become one of the big five among saxophonists, the rest of whom are Coleman Hawkins, Ben Webster, Lester

Young, and Parker. Even more important, he belongs in that small collection of jazz musicians who, lyric poets all, function closest to the heart of the music—such men as Webster, Herschel Evans, Sidney Bechet, Buck Clayton, Bill Coleman, Vic Dickenson, Red Allen, Pee Wee Russell, Charlie Mingus, and John Lewis. And within *that* collection, he has joined Bechet—who tutored him extensively on the soprano saxophone in the early thirties, and who had a good deal to do with his ultimate style—in bringing jazz perilously close to a sentimental music.

Hodges' bent toward sweetness did not emerge until the mid-thirties, when he began recording, with Ellington, a series of slow solos based on tunes like "In a Sentimental Mood" and "Passion Flower." On such occasions, which he still indulges in, Hodges employs a tone that falls between the country-cream sound of Tab Smith and the flutings of Willie Smith. It is a tone that seems to be draped over the notes like a lap robe. Hodges does little improvising in these ballads. Instead, he issues fulsome statements of the melody, languorous legato phrases, and long glissandi topped by an almost unctuous vibrato. Because of their richness and lack of melodic variation, they sometimes suggest that Hodges could easily be slipped into a Guy Lombardo saxophone section. Hodges' Edgar Guest strain is generally well concealed, though, and it is nowhere in sight when he plays the blues, which have long provided his basic materials. Here, Hodges moves up onto his toes and grows alternately oblique and goatlike. His tone shrinks, occasionally even becoming dry and sharp, he uses more notes, his vibrato steadies, and his impeccable sense of rhythmic placement—how long to tarry on this or

that note, just where to break a pause, which notes
(if any) should be emphasized in a run—is put to
work. In a medium-tempo blues—the speed at
which Hodges most often jells—the result is a mixture of lullaby delicacy and gentlemanly emotion.
Suggesting but never commanding, Hodges may
start such a solo by sounding four descending notes,
which are placed on successive beats and connected
by an almost inaudible threadlike hum, as if he
were two instrumentalists in one—the first playing
the four notes and the second providing background choir chords. After a short pause, he will ap-
plaud his own natty lightness by repeating the pattern, adding a single offbeat note and increasing his
volume. Then he will double his volume and deliver
a soaring exclamation, which he will sustain only
long enough to make it ring, and end it with an unexpectedly soft blue note. He may start this cry
once more, break it off with a complex descending-
ascending-descending run, and, all delicacy gone,
launch into a second chorus with a short, heavy riff,
which will either be repeated, with variations, or
give way to several rapid staccato phrases. He will
close his solo by returning to a whispered three-or-
four-note passage, which floats serenely at one, slips
past, and offhandedly disappears. Hodges' blues
solos are child's play in comparison with Parker's.
But they are also classic balancings of tone, dynamics, rhythm, and choice of notes. There is no extraneous matter, and no thinness. There is no opac-
ity. It is *mot-juste* improvising, and because of its
basic understatement it illuminates completely the
elegance and purity of the blues. At faster tempos,
Hodges relies almost entirely on his rhythmic capac-
ities. The solos he thus achieves are often the quint-
essence of "jump" playing. They move on and

sometimes ahead of the beat, and there is a good deal of tasteful repetition. At the same time, Hodges' rhythmic attack is mainly implied; he rolls rather than tramps toward his destination, which, in contrast to the majority of jazz soloists, he always reaches.

Hodges is in tonic condition in "Side by Side: Duke Ellington and Johnny Hodges" and "Blues A-Plenty: Johnny Hodges and His Orchestra" (Verve). Of the nine titles on the first record (four blues, four standards, and an Ellington original), three were recorded by Hodges, Ellington, Harry Edison, and a rhythm section including Jo Jones. These three are notable for Hodges' strict jump choruses in "Stompy Jones" and for all Ellington's solos, which are given uncommon lift by Jones, particularly in "Stompy Jones." Edison, despite similar assists, remains Johnny-one-note throughout, and it is difficult to see why he was matched with Ellington and Hodges. On hand with Hodges on the rest of the record are Roy Eldridge, Ben Webster, Lawrence Brown, Wendell Marshall, Billy Strayhorn, and Jones. "Big Shoe" is similar to those attractive medium-tempo blues that made up most of Hodges' small-band recordings in the forties. Eldridge, in his Sunday-best, delivers two perfect choruses bracketed between exhilarating but controlled dashes into the upper register and deep-down growls. Hodges' second chorus is largely smears. "Just a Memory" and "Let's Fall in Love," which are done in medium tempo, include gentle statements from all the horns, who demonstrate precisely how to construct solos with a beginning, a middle, and a climactic end.

Four of the nine numbers in "Blue A-Plenty," which is played by the leader plus Eldridge, Webster, Vic Dickenson, Strayhorn, Jimmy Woode, and Sam Woodyard, are better-than-average Hodges rhapsodies. He neither weeps nor moans, and in "Satin Doll" he delivers much of the melody in a blunt lower-register manner that suggests Webster. (Hodges taught Webster much of what he knows.) The rest of the numbers are excellent blues. Most remarkable of all is the long medium-tempo "Reeling and Rocking," which, after the ensemble, is given over to a succession of choruses by Hodges, Dickenson (followed by a restatement of the melody), Webster, Eldridge, and Hodges again that are consummate lyrical jazz improvisations. Each soloist, his clichés left at home, is in peak shape, and the results are five studies in the blues that are singular for Hodges' way of seemingly attacking his notes from behind (first solo) and then for his landing on them in an almost soundless slow motion (second solo); for Dickenson's jumble of smears, growls, knucklings, and swaggers at the outset of his second chorus; for Webster's sliding, hymnlike statement; and for Eldridge's reined-in fury. This is one of those rare jazz performances that defy all faddishness, fickleness, and foolishness.

Made in France

ONE OF the least admirable faults of both the big and the little recording companies during the past decade has been their refusal, despite generally booming times and a small but ready-made market, to reissue in any quantity or with any logic the vast amount of superior jazz in their vaults. (This is not to mention the plethora of third-rate new recordings and the extraordinary lack of taste with which most of them are packaged.) There are a few notable exceptions. Columbia has brought out essential collections of Bessie Smith, Louis Armstrong, Bix Beiderbecke, Count Basie, Fletcher Henderson, Red Nichols, and the small Benny Goodman groups, and is assembling comprehensive L.P.s by Mildred Bailey, Teddy Wilson, and Billie Holiday. There has been no word, though, of such sterling but less celebrated performers as Henry Allen, Earl Hines, Cab Calloway, and Cootie Williams, or of a host of fine recordings by blues singers and miscellaneous small groups. Victor has been far more fitful. Skimpy and/or often ill-chosen collections by Lionel Hampton, Frankie Newton, Muggsy Spanier, Armstrong, Fats Waller, and Duke Ellington have appeared and disappeared, but Sidney Bechet, Tommy Ladnier, Dickie Wells, Bill Coleman, Hines, Jelly Roll Morton, the small Ellington and Goodman groups, and, again, the blues singers remain largely unavailable. True, Victor began an ambitious reissue program five or six years ago, but it was given up not long afterward because of allegedly slow sales—despite the fact that the series was bought up so assiduously that it has already become a collectors' item. Decca has been distressingly lackadaisical. It has released spotty Armstrong and Jimmy Lunceford albums, a good Basie one, and several ineptly assembled history-of-jazz-type anthologies. However, Chick Webb, Fletcher and Horace Henderson, and Hines have been ignored, to say nothing of Andy Kirk, Jay McShann, Lucky Millinder, Claude Hopkins, and Jabbo Smith. Decca is also keeping unto itself the recordings of the famous 1944 Metropolitan Opera House concert at which Armstrong, Roy Eldridge,

Jack Teagarden, Art Tatum, Sid Catlett, Billie Holiday, Mildred Bailey, and Lionel Hampton appeared. Of the smaller labels, which necessarily operate on a narrow economic margin, only Riverside has scattered largess about, by reissuing all of the 1938 Jelly Roll Morton Library of Congress recordings, some of the Solo Art boogie-woogie numbers, a lot of Paramount and Gennett recordings, some of them pretty academic, and, most recently, the best (and worst) of the Hot Record Society label. Commodore has made sporadic attempts to reinstate part of its invaluable list, while Blue Note, the oldest all-jazz label, has done almost nothing about its superb boogie-woogie recordings and the classic sides made in the early forties by Frankie Newton, J. C. Higginbotham, Bechet, Sidney de Paris, Charlie Christian, Edmond Hall, Ben Webster, Vic Dickenson, James P. Johnson, and Catlett.

These observations have been provoked by the ironic but welcome intelligence that a fair proportion of these neglected materials is now available on various French labels, and can be purchased readily and cheaply by mail and American check—plus minor shipping and duty charges—from a large record shop, the Palais de la Radio et du Disque, at 30 Boulevard des Italiens, Paris, IX. Only a handful of the material on the forty or so reissue L.P.s available at the Palais can be found over here; most of it has been out of print for ten or twenty years. This includes most of the Lionel Hampton small-band recordings (1937-41), Johnny Dodds (1928-29), Armstrong (1925-47), Billie Holiday (1933-41), Chick Webb (1934-39), McKinney's Cotton Pickers (1929-31), Luis Russell (1929-30), Bill Coleman (1936-37), and Bechet (1932-41).

One of the most gratifying of these records is

"Bill Coleman" (FOLP), which includes ten numbers made in Paris with various groups consisting of both Belgian and French musicians (Django Reinhardt and Stéphane Grappelly) and American ones (Herman Chittison and Wilson Myers). Of all the less celebrated ghostlike musicians who regularly pass through jazz, Coleman, who is now fifty-six, is one of the most undervalued. (He is well known, though, in France, where he has lived since 1948.) One reason for this has been the footloose nature of his career. After playing trumpet in New York in the late twenties and early thirties with Luis Russell, Cecil Scott, and Charlie Johnson, Coleman dodged back and forth between this country, Europe, India, and Egypt. During the war, he reappeared here, hopping from Benny Carter to Teddy Wilson to Andy Kirk to Noble Sissle to Mary Lou Williams to John Kirby, and then was off to the Philippines and Japan before settling in France. As a result, his recording activity has been catch-as-catch-can. Aside from "Bill Coleman," which includes ten of the eighteen sides made under his leadership, Coleman's output during the height of his career (1935-45) consisted largely of some sessions with Dickie Wells and Fats Waller, a few obscure Teddy Wilson dates (one of them as a member of a band that included Benny Morton, Bud Freeman, Charlie Christian, and Edmond Hall, and that provided gorgeous backing for the intrusive patent-leather singing of Eddy Howard), and infrequent pickup recordings done for fly-by-night labels. Finally, Coleman, whose style is singularly subtle, had to contend in his prime with such extroverts as Cootie Williams, Armstrong, Eldridge, Charlie Shavers, and Harry Edison. Even Buck Clayton, a contemporary and peer of Coleman's who has a

Made in France 131

similar style, has become well known only recently.

Coleman's playing, which owes something to Armstrong and perhaps to Red Allen and Jabbo Smith, has slowed down appreciably since the war, but on these recordings it is miraculous. It is the exact opposite of the sluggish, the crude, the unfinished, the heavy, and the pompous. It is poignant but not sweet, gentle but not effete, graceful but not fancy. It exhibits the sort of degravitational agility associated with a clarinetist, a flutist, or a pianist. (Coleman would have been a match for the mercurial patterns of Tatum.) Most trumpet players never conquer the insistent brassiness of their instrument, but Coleman's unique tone (Beiderbecke's, on cornet, comes closest to it) sometimes suggests light bells, sometimes lucent silk. Long before the idea became fashionable, Coleman was using complex unbroken melodic lines and the sort of devious rhythmic attack associated with bebop. Because of their dancing slipperiness, Coleman's improvisations—particularly at fast tempos—are difficult to pin down. After playing a chorus of the melody in an intent legato fashion, he may slip directly into the upper register, achieving a glancing falsetto quality, dart downward before one even realizes where he has been, and dissolve into a smooth, fat phrase, then race up and down between the middle and high registers, shoot upwards, and slope away into a decelerating passage, his notes falling just behind the beat. Coleman never seems to breathe, and after such a floating interlude he immediately pours through another series of arabesques, involving all the registers, and then pumps down the melody itself as a signpost for the succeeding soloist.

At least half of the selections on the Coleman record, which has three blues, some standards like

"After You've Gone," "Coquette," and "Indiana," and Django Reinhardt's "Swing Guitars," are first-rate. "After You've Gone," made with Herman Chittison and a bass player, is an up-tempo investigation full of stunning breaks and inter-register leaps. "I Ain't Got Nobody" and "Swing Guitars" are, possibly because of Reinhardt's presence, admirably relaxed medium-tempo numbers in which Coleman seems to bask in his own sounds. The same is true of the blues, all of them slow or medium slow, including the mildly famous "Bill Coleman Blues," a long series of delicate, muted choruses accompanied only by Reinhardt. The rhythm sections have a cardboard resiliency, but this doesn't bother Coleman, who usually gives the impression of being able to play at peak inspiration without any accompaniment at all.

Another valuable recording from the Palais is "Luis Russell and His Orchestra" (Odéon). Its fourteen sides were made in New York in 1929 and 1930 by a band that includes, with minor additions and subtractions, Red Allen, Coleman (one number), J. C. Higginbotham, Charlie Holmes (alto saxophone), Teddy Hill (tenor saxophone), Russell (piano), Will Johnson (guitar), Pops Foster, and Paul Barbarin (drums). The Russell band helped pioneer the modern rhythm section (guitar and string bass in place of banjo and tuba) and was perhaps the hardest-driving group of its time. Its arrangements are fairly intricate. Riffs are handed back and forth by the brass and reeds, often in a call-and-response pattern. There are curious, almost rhythmless interludes in which one instrument solos against chords played by the rest of the band, tight unison ensembles strikingly similar to those now fashionable among the funky players, and plenty of breaks. But there is also ample solo space. Allen had by then begun to move away from Armstrong's influence, and was firing off, in an edgy tone, a lot of blue notes and wild, searching phrases that generally got where they were going. Coleman's single solo is astonishing; it is already the later Coleman minus shellac. Higginbotham is also surprising. He had already developed a galelike attack—replete with crazy runs, high-register shouts and smears, and complex many-noted phrases—that only Dickie Wells and Jimmy Knepper have matched since. The best of the selections, which are somewhat uneven, include a slow, spooky "New Call of the Freaks," "Doctor Blues," "Saratoga Shout," and "Song of the Swanee." All of these are free of the slightly frantic quality of the remaining numbers and are indicative of the supple approach that was to become the badge of the great Harlem bands five or six years later.

In 1932 and 1940-41, Sidney Bechet recorded approximately three dozen sides for Victor under the title of "Sidney Bechet and His New Orleans Feetwarmers." With the exception of the demonic 1932 session, they were pickup recordings that used not New Orleans men but swing musicians like Catlett, Sandy Williams, Sidney de Paris, Allen, Higginbotham, Hines, Rex Stewart, and Dickenson. Accordingly, the ensembles are informal and the solos plentiful and excellent. Twenty-three of the Feetwarmer sessions have been brought together on "Sidney Bechet" and "Sidney Bechet: Blues in the Air" (RCA). These records can also be had from Paris. The first record has eight memorable selections, including all four of the De Paris-Williams-

Catlett dates and two of the Stewart-Hines-Baby Dodds ones, while the second record offers, in addition to the weakest of the 1932 numbers and some lacklustre 1941 efforts with such as Henry Goodwin (trumpet) and Charlie Shavers, three of the four metallic, explosive Allen-Higginbotham-J. C. Heard numbers. Bechet's inspiration works throughout in direct ratio to the quality of his cohorts.

Bechet reappears in four of the eleven recordings made in New York in the fall of 1938 by Ladnier, Mezz Mezzrow, De Paris, James P. Johnson, Teddy Bunn, and Zutty Singleton, among others. These have been collected in France on "Really the Blues" (FELP), and resemble, despite Mezzrow, the Feetwarmer dates. Indeed, there are two eloquent slow blues, "If You See Me Comin'" and "Really the Blues," that haven't even begun to weather.

Yes Yes Yes Yes

WHEN I heard that Ida Cox, the legendary seventy-year-old blues singer, had been located in Knoxville after a long search, that she was still in excellent voice, and that she had been persuaded by Chris Albertson, of Riverside Records, to come to New York and make her first recording in over twenty years, I contacted Albertson and arranged to have a talk with Miss Cox before the recording session and to drop in at the studio and witness the start of her new career. On the appointed day, I went over to the Paramount Hotel, on West Forty-sixth Street, where Riverside has its offices and where Miss Cox was staying, and was ushered up to her room by Albertson, who introduced us. Tallish, straight-backed, gray-haired, and handsomely proportioned, Miss Cox was wearing schoolmarm spectacles, a smart brown dress, and red bedroom slippers, and looked at least a decade younger than her age.

"Take that nice chair in the corner, honey," she told me firmly. "And put your feet up on the bed and be comfortable."

I asked Miss Cox if she was uneasy about the recording.

"Lord, I haven't thought about it since I finally decided to do it," she replied. "At first, I felt I just couldn't. My health haven't been so good since I had a stroke in Buffalo in 1944. I walked out on a night-club floor there and it look like everything left me, everything went black. I haven't sung a note since, and I do thank God for sparing me this long. Of course, I'm here now, and I mean to do the best I can, but then I'm going back home—*whoom*, like that. I'll record some of my own blues—'Fore Day Creep,' 'Moanin' Groanin' Blues,' 'Cherry Pickin' Blues,' 'Graveyard Dream Blues.' I remember the words pretty well, even if most everything else—people and all what I've done in my life—it vanishes away."

Would Miss Cox tell me about her early, or first career?

"I was born in Cedartown, Georgia," she said. "When I was fourteen, I ran away and joined a minstrel show, the Black and Tan. I sang blues and ragtime songs, like 'Put Your Arms Around Me, Honey' and an old, old one I learned from my brother, 'Hard, Oh Lord.' Oh, how does that go?" Miss Cox put her hand to her forehead, sat silent for several moments, and then sang, in a quiet, clear voice, "Hard, hard, ain't it hard, Oh Lord,/ To love and can't be loved./Hard, hard, ain't it hard, Oh Lord,/To love and can't be loved." She stopped and laughed. "Now, I mean that's been *years* ago. Then I went with the Rabbit Foot Minstrels and the Florida Blossom Minstrels and into vaudeville. Jelly Roll Morton—he was a good-lookin' light-skinned boy—played for me at the Eight One Theatre, on Decatur Street, in Atlanta, and one of his tunes, 'Jelly Roll Blues,' was my first big success. I worked at the Plantation, in Chicago, with King Oliver and Louis Armstrong. Oliver was fat and plain, and almost as homely as I am. After that, I sang in every state in the Union. I had one of the most lovely colored shows on the road—a beautiful chorus line. I got to know everybody, and worked with the biggest portion of them. Bessie Smith was an old, old friend and everybody loved her, which was why they was so shocked when she died in that accident. Of course, she *did* have enemies. Who don't? She was a very high-tempered person, and she didn't take anything from anybody. But she was a good girl, on the whole. Billie Holiday, she was a fine person, too. Always smiling. But her ways were her own. That's a girl's life, it seemed to me, was just snapped away from foolishness. She was a deserving person. Ethel Waters is another dear friend, and Duke Ellington. One time, I was playing Houston, and Ellington and his band was sitting around a table out front. I went out after I was done and kissed him—just fooling, you know. When I got home, my husband like to all but knock my block off. Some crazy little things happen in your life."

Yes Yes Yes Yes

There was a rap on the door, and Albertson, who had returned to his office, came in and told Miss Cox it was time for rehearsals.

I thanked her and said I'd see her at the recording studio.

"That would be nice, honey," she said. "You come, please."

The studio, on the eighth floor of Radio City Music Hall, turned out to be a spacious buff-colored room filled with microphones, timpani, bass drums, tomtoms, chimes, vibraphones, a small Wurlitzer organ, a grand piano, musicians, and interested observers. Miss Cox, a white sweater drawn around her shoulders, was seated near the piano, her hands folded placidly in her lap and a benign expression on her face, while a handful of photographers hovered about her. Albertson greeted me. "Coleman Hawkins overslept," he said. "We're waiting on him, and we've substituted Sammy Price on piano for Jesse Crump, who couldn't make it from the Coast." On the opposite side of the room, a loud argument was going on between Price and the rest of Miss Cox's accompanists—Roy Eldridge, Milt Hinton, and Jo Jones—about the whereabouts of Jabbo Smith.

"I saw him two years ago in Newark," Eldridge said to Price. "And he was playing trombone, too!"

"Jabbo Smith?" Price exclaimed. "Why, he's dead, man! Here, I'll bet you a hundred dollars."

"Dead? He lives in Milwaukee," Jones said. "I've got his address right in my book."

"Put up your money," Price said to Eldridge.

At this point, the studio door opened, and Hawkins, his eyes puffy with sleep, a black felt hat low on his head, walked quickly in. One of Miss Cox's blues, "Hard Times," was chosen for the first number, and after the arrangement had been sketched out, Miss Cox walked up to a microphone, tilted her head slightly back, bent her shoulders, and dropped her hands to her sides. Price played the introduction, and Miss Cox began to sing, in a round, serene, low voice, while Eldridge growled distantly in the background:

"I never seen such real hard times before.
No, I never seen such real hard times before.
The wolf keeps walkin' all around my door.

"They howl all night long, and they moan till
   the break of day.
They howl all night long, and they moan till
   the break of day.
They seem to know my good man gone away."

After two more choruses of singing, Hawkins soloed and Miss Cox exclaimed, in double time, "Yes yes yes yes yes, talk to me, talk to me," and then returned to the lyric: "I'm a big fat momma, got the meat shakin' on my bones . . ."

Before I left, three tunes later, I told Miss Cox she sounded better than ever.

"Why, that's lovely, honey," she said, beaming. "And I thank you, I thank you so much."

Sonny Greer

AT WORK, most modern jazz musicians appear to be suffering from shock. They adopt blank, masklike faces, stand rigidly still, and rarely speak to one another, let alone the audience. The only proof they are not hallucinations is the sound that comes from their instruments, and even this isn't always conclusive. Twenty years ago jazz musicians usually mirrored every emotion they were undergoing. Drummers, in particular, went further by adding the icing of guileless showmanship. They twirled their sticks or tossed them into the air, generally in time to the music, smiled expansively or grimaced (Kansas Fields always looked on the verge of tears), snapped their heads about militaristically, and manipulated the wire brushes like skilled house painters. The three consummate showmen-drummers were Sidney Catlett, Jo Jones, and Sonny Greer. (Gene Krupa and Buddy Rich were showoffs.) Now that Catlett is dead and Greer in partial obscurity, only Jones remains consistently on view. A week ago, however, Greer, who is sixty, appeared in full bloom at a Duke Ellington Society concert given in the Carnegie Recital Hall.

Greer quit Ellington in 1951, after thirty-odd years—a departure that has left a permanent gap in the band. A flattish, dapper man with a thin, tongue-in-cheek face and a patent-leather air, Greer epitomized the easy elegance of the Ellington band. He was generally enthroned slightly above and to the rear of his colleagues, amid a resplendent array of equipment that included a couple of timpani, chimes, and a J. Arthur Rank gong. For all his outward grace and polish, though, Greer's style was and is strictly homemade. He is only a fair technician (his time is uneven, sometimes he is overbearing, and he misses strokes) and he has never been much of a soloist. Indeed, he often gives the impression that he is *testing* rather than playing his drums. He moves ceaselessly back and forth between his cymbals, sampling their centers, drops in sudden experimental offbeats on the cowbell (an unfortunately outmoded bit of drum paraphernalia), rustles his high-hat cymbals ominously and then clamps them shut with a *whussht*, inserts crescendo snare-drum rolls, sounds jumbo beats on his bass drum or settles into steady lackadaisical afterbeats on the snare rims. Greer's showmanship accents all this. A mock-serious look will dissolve into a broad smile, a wide-eyed expression into a sleepy one. An eyes-right-or-left head motion punctuates every number. After twirling a stick faster than a propeller, he may rear back in amazement at his prowess. Greer is sound and motion in miraculous counterpoint.

With Greer were Clark Terry on trumpet and flügelhorn, Hilton Jefferson, Wendell Marshall, and a ringer, Jimmy Jones, on piano. Two singers—Betty Roché and Ozzie Bailey—also appeared. Eight of the twenty numbers, most of them by Ellington and/or Billy Strayhorn, were taken up with vocals. Bailey was surprisingly attractive, in a thin, valentine way, while Miss Roché was calculated and tart. Aside from the four group numbers, Jefferson, Terry, and Jones each had two selections to themselves, and Greer had one. This was an up-tempo version of "Caravan," in which he started softly with his hands on the tomtoms, gradually increased the volume, picked up two sticks in his right hand, pitted this hand against his still empty left hand (much rattling and whapping), tucked his sticks nonchalantly under his right arm, returned to his hands, reduced his volume, and closed with a jarring bass-drum *frump*. During the rest of the afternoon, Greer ticked off all of his tricks—wire brushes on a large tomtom behind Jones, mallet crescendos during the ensembles, spinning sticks, and casual, off-beat rimshots. In fact, Greer managed to convey the notion that he was still supporting the entire Ellington band—insouciance, white jackets, the Duke, and all.

Young Werther

BARRING THE BLUES and Duke Ellington, jazz has never bothered its head much about content. It has been far more concerned with such technical matters as improvisation, timbre, tone, attack, and, lately, form. Thus, the outstanding thing about Miles Davis is not his style but its genuine, though elusive, content. This style consists largely of carefully modulated mannerisms. In the slow ballads, Davis, using a mute, buzzes rhythmically and persistently at the melody, like a bluebottle. In the easy medium-tempo numbers, often blues played open-horn, he irregularly issues long, thick-voiced single notes that are neither quite on nor quite off pitch, brief, stabbed notes, and little broken-off runs that suggest unfinished staircases. In the fast uphill tempos, his come-as-you-are technique races along just behind his ideas, never quite catching up. The results are feminine forays into the upper registers, curiously heavy arpeggios, and a nutant melodic line. Of late, Davis has added to these approaches an almost funereal legato style in the middle and lower registers. These young-Werther ruminations most clearly reveal the content of Davis's music—a view of things that is brooding, melancholy, perhaps self-pitying, and extremely close to the sentimental. It is, except for certain aspects of Johnny Hodges and Sidney Bechet, a new flavor in jazz.

Davis's recent recordings as a soloist with various big bands led by the arranger-composer Gil Evans have had a good deal to do with this revelation. Evans is an ingenious orchestrator whose often unique and not necessarily jazzlike instrumental combinations give off a moody, caressive air. Unavoidably, Davis has taken on some of the colors and shapes of Evans's work. This was strikingly evident last Friday in Carnegie Hall, when Davis and Evans offered their first concert collaboration. The concert was something of a jumble. Five numbers were played by Davis's quintet (Hank Mobley, Wynton Kelly, Paul Chambers, and Jimmy Cobb), two were joint efforts by the quintet and Evans's twenty-piece group, and four were by Davis and the group, with Evans conducting. Davis the stylist was brilliantly visible in the quintet numbers, which included a slow muted ballad, a leisurely middle-tempo open-horn blues, and a couple of agitated up-tempo pieces, none of them identified. (A laconic, weed-like figure, Davis never lets his audiences know that he knows they're there; he neither speaks to them nor looks at them nor even plays to them.) Davis the philosopher emerged in two of his numbers with Evans. These were Evans's reworking of part of Joaquín Rodrigo's "Concierto de Aranjuez," for guitar and orchestra, and Evans's variations on a *saeta*, or Spanish folk song. In the first, which lasted better than fifteen minutes, Davis, backed by Evans's mistiest palette, improvised on the guitar part, reveling in declamatory phrases, low, round-shouldered notes, and simple embellishments of the melody, which drips with flamencan dolor. Indeed, Davis was misery distilled. The *saeta* was a short, delightful piece in which Davis, framed by marching drums, tambourines, a harp, and trumpets,

Young Werther

issued a series of prolonged, fluttering muezzin calls with bent-note endings. Davis was by far the most impressive performer onstage. Mobley and Kelly soloed rhetorically, and Cobb, who also worked with Evans's group, was adequate. Although Evans's men occasionally stumbled, they managed to sustain much of the silken roll of his music, upon which Evans himself—a thin spidery figure—seemed to jubilantly bob.

Trove

THERE'S NO gainsaying that Hollywood's cheerful desecration of the arts has been all but impartial. Literature, music, and the dance—let alone the film itself—have been sterilized with equal vigor and concentration. But jazz, which didn't reach Hollywood until the late twenties, is an exception. To be sure, countless full-length burlesques of the music exist, among them those oleaginous biographies in which Danny Kaye appears as Red Nichols and Kirk Douglas as Bix Beiderbecke. Nonetheless, while Hollywood's right hand was fashioning such vaudeville items, its left hand was turning out untold numbers of invaluable jazz shorts. Though almost invariably hoked up with dancers, Uncle Toms, precious photography, and costumes ranging from bellhops' uniforms to leopard-skin togas, these films often contain excellent jazz—some of it, in fact, by groups that were never recorded elsewhere. One celebrated example is Elmer Snowden's 1932 Small's Paradise band. A disheartening number of these shorts have been lost or have simply disintegrated, but a good many others have been rescued by valiant collectors. Recently, one of these collectors, Ernest R. Smith, a fast-talking, thirty-seven-year-old advertising executive, exhibited, as the first of three programs, eleven jazz shorts (all but two from his collection) in a small auditorium in Freedom House.

The program was opened and closed by two extraordinary films—*St. Louis Blues*, a short made in 1929 with Bessie Smith, and *Jammin' the Blues*, photographed in 1944 by Gjon Mili. Miss Smith plays what appears to be a lady of the night who is knocked down and robbed by her man. (The story lines of these shorts were never more than transparent.) Most of her picture, which is an odd mixture of realism and soap opera, is given over to a scene in a night club, where Miss Smith, propped drunkenly but magisterially against the bar, sings a monumental version of the title song, accompanied by part of Fletcher Henderson's band and the Hall-Johnson choir—a combination that lends an operatic atmosphere to the number. (Joe Smith, Henderson's great, ruby-toned cornetist, is also visible and audible.) Parts of *Jammin' the Blues* are arty, but the picture is largely a straightforward record of such men as Lester Young, Harry Edison, Jo Jones, and Sid Catlett playing a couple of blues and a standard. Included are superb shots of Young's lidded, moonlike face, a bassist's bony, concave fingers, and Catlett obliquely from the rear, his sequoia self swaying slowly from side to side, his left arm hanging limp, wire brush in hand.

In between these pictures, Smith ran off two Ellington shorts—*Black and Tan Fantasy* (1929) and *Symphony in Black* (1935)—that are, despite their theatrics, filled with commendable solos by

Trove

Bubber Miley, Johnny Hodges, Tricky Sam Nanton, Cootie Williams, and Lawrence Brown. Moreover, in the second one, Billie Holiday, in perfect voice and looking as fresh as a butterball, sings a couple of choruses of the blues. The Ellington shorts were almost matched by a Louis Armstrong film, *Rhapsody in Black and Blue* (1932), in which Armstrong, at the height of his powers and dressed in a leopard skin, gets off a fast "I'll Be Glad When You're Dead You Rascal You" and a fascinating "Shine," sung and played in both middle and uptempos. The rest of the evening was more absorbing sociologically than musically. Armstrong reappeared, both live and animated, in a Betty Boop cartoon, also entitled *I'll Be Glad When You're Dead You Rascal You*, which is so tasteless it is funny. (At one point, Armstrong's huge, mugging, disembodied head chases a tiny animated missionary type across an endless plain.) The program was completed by five so-called "soundies," which were three-minute films made in the early forties for jukeboxlike machines equipped with small screens. Two were by Gene Krupa's band (1941-42), with Roy Eldridge and Anita O'Day, and three by Fats Waller (1941 and 1942), who, surrounded by a gaggle of beauties, rubbers and jowls his way through "Ain't Misbehavin'," "Honeysuckle Rose," and "The Joint is Jumpin'."

All but two of the fifteen or so films in Smith's second showing, which included shorts, sequences from shorts and full-length pictures, and soundies, were from his collection. The best things were often the most tantalizing. In an excerpt from *After Seven*, a short done in 1928 with Chick Webb's band, there was a single, fleeting glimpse of Webb himself—peering, tiny and spidery, over the top of his drums—and a great deal of James Barton, singing and dancing in blackface. A Count Basie short, made in 1939 by the greatest of the Basie bands, was centered on the Delta Rhythm Boys and on let's-get-it-over-with footage of the band doing three lightning numbers that included solos—and good shots—of Harry Edison, Buck Clayton, Jo Jones, Walter Page, Don Byas, and Basie, dressed in a Glen-plaid horse blanket. *Bundle of Blues*, a 1933 Ellington short, was less frustrating. Although most of the film was taken up with poetic shots of a rain-streaked window, an axe stuck in a wet stump, a slave cabin in the rain, rain on leaves, and rain on a pond, while an invisible Ivie Anderson sang "Stormy Weather" (what a good singer she was!), there were satisfying closeups and statements from Cootie Williams, Tricky Sam Nanton, Freddy Guy, and Sonny Greer. Best of all was a 1940 short, filmed in the vanished Café Society Uptown. Albert Ammons and Pete Johnson buffaloed their way through "Boogie Woogie Dream," Lena Horne sang a blues, exhibiting the finest teeth ever owned by a human being, and Teddy Wilson's small band (Emmett Berry, Benny Morton, Jimmy Hamilton, and J. C. Heard) played an exemplary medium-tempo blues.

The rest of the evening was either square and funny or given over to maddening snippets. The squarest moments came during shorts by Artie Shaw (1939) and Stan Kenton (1945). In the first a commentator anatomized swing ("a pounding, ensenuating rhythm") while Shaw and Buddy Rich, looking barely hatched, did a duet, and in the second a leviathan Kenton ensemble (six trumpets, four trombones, five saxophones, four rhythm) dem-

onstrated how to play for the millennium. The snippets were sometimes dazzling: Cab Calloway shouting and shimmying "Minnie the Moocher" while
Cozy Cole, Jonah Jones, Mousie Randolph, and
Danny Barker graced the background; Jack Teagarden singing and playing "Basin Street Blues" in
1938 (shots of the Mississippi and the Mardi Gras);
part of a 1946 "March of Time," showing the Art
Tatum Trio on Fifty-second Street and an Eddie
Condon group with Dave Tough, his face cavernous
and haunted, his arms like thongs; and another
Basie short, made by his sextet in 1950, that
included two superb selections by Billie Holiday
("God Bless the Child" and a blues), and half a
dozen boogie-woogie numbers by Sugar Chile Robin-
son, a ten-year-old prodigy whom Basie treated as if
Sugar Chile were Charlie McCarthy and he were
W. C. Fields.

The final showing numbered two dozen shorts,
snippets from shorts, brief films done around 1950
for television, and soundies. Since Smith's collection,
like all treasure-troves, has a bottom, the program
was pretty raggle-tagggle. There were lots of vocals
by Louis Jordan, Peggy Lee, Sarah Vaughan, June
Christy, Billy Eckstine (with his 1946 big band,
which had Gene Ammons and Art Blakey, both of
them visible), and Fats Waller, as well as instrumentals by the clean-cut, 4-H bands of Glen Gray,
Buddy Rich, Larry Clinton, and Stan Kenton. But
the scattered exceptions were wonderful. In a couple of 1942 Louis Armstrong soundies, done with
the last of his big bands, Armstrong sang "Shine"
and played a fine short solo, and the late Velma
Middleton, straining the joists, sang and danced
"Swingin' on Nothin'." The high points of the Arm-

strong selections, though, were several fleeting shots of Sid Catlett, who was between jobs with Benny Goodman and Teddy Wilson's Café Society Uptown band. A monumentlike figure behind his drums, his eyes revealing the slightly malevolent expression they sometimes assumed when he was concentrating, he could be seen, in a last glimpse, casually spinning a drumstick through the air (a blurred-moon effect) with his right hand while his left descended like an enormous fly swatter on his hi-hat cymbals. Of equal value were a number by Al Cooper and his Savoy Sultans, a semi-legendary and very hot Harlem band from the late thirties, and two short television films by Jack Teagarden (made in company with Ray Bauduc and Charlie Teagarden), who fashioned first-rate solos in "That's A-Plenty" and "The Jack Armstrong Blues." Three kick-the-can Lionel Hampton big-band numbers (1950–52) were saved by the spectacle of Milt Buckner, a round, bespectacled frog, who played the up-tempo "Cobb's Idea" with such fervor that he cleared both the piano stool and the floor on each beat. The usual Uncle Tom effects were visible during the evening (Armstrong's "Shine" opened with two Negroes shining a huge shoe—an unpardonable visual pun, since the title of the song is simply a pejorative term for a Negro) and reached an apogee in "Sophisticated Lady," a 1951 Duke Ellington short, in which the alto saxophonist Willie Smith, who is a nearly white Negro, was shown not *in* the band but as a soloist standing well in front of it, his chair in the saxophone section remaining resoundingly empty throughout the picture. This sort of discretion and thoughtfulness must make white-supremacists weak with gratitude.

Not long after Smith's film showings, I was invited to a preview of a taped one-hour television show called "Chicago and All That Jazz," a spirited attempt to re-create the jazz played in Chicago from the mid-teens until 1929, when the music moved its headquarters to New York. About three-quarters of the program was given over to performances by Kid Ory, Red Allen, Jack Teagarden, Lil Hardin Armstrong, Johnny St. Cyr, Meade Lux Lewis, Blossom Seeley, Al Minns, and Leon James. The remaining quarter included an array of striking and often extremely rare film clips from old feature films, newsreels, shorts, and home movies, which offered glimpses of, among others, Bessie Smith, Mamie Smith, Louis Armstrong, Jimmie Noone, and Bix Beiderbecke. My host was Ernest Smith, who has spent all his spare time and cash during the past five years collecting jazz-and-film memorabilia, stills from films concerned with jazz, and the films themselves. As a result of this activity, Smith probably knows as much about the subject as anyone alive. Smith's collection of stills, about a thousand strong, is unmatched, while his collection of films, which includes seven or eight features and some eighty shorts, is surpassed only by that of John Baker, a Columbus, Ohio, collector who owns well over three hundred items. I learned these things shortly after the screening, when I had a talk with Smith at his apartment, at Lexington Avenue and Ninetieth Street.

Once I was settled in Smith's workroom, a small, immaculate box filled with reels of film, cardboard files, huge loose-leaf notebooks, and film reference books, I asked him how he had become involved with "Chicago and All That Jazz." Smith, who is a short, amiable, firmly built man with a soft aquiline nose and dark hair, told me that N.B.C. had approached him late in June, and that he had worked closely with an admirable woman named Helen Kiok, who was the show's film researcher. "They asked me if I knew of anything on Eddie Lang or Bix Beiderbecke or Mamie Smith," Smith said, putting out a cigarette and taking a brownie from a dish at his elbow. "I didn't, but things got started when Len Kunstadt, a jazz-collector friend of mine who lives in Brooklyn, told Helen that Tony Parenti, the clarinetist, had a home movie of Lang, with Tommy and Jimmy Dorsey, taken in a recording studio. Helen reached Parenti, but unfortunately the film wasn't used, even though it's great—Lang standing by a piano with the Dorseys off to one side. More important, Parenti said that the twenties bandleader Boyd Senter—Boyd Senter and His Senterpedes he was known as—might have some film or stills. But where was Senter? As it happened, on my way to Kalamazoo by train early last summer I had got off in Detroit and bought an apple and all the local papers—a research habit I've gotten into. This was before I'd even heard of the television show. I found a tiny ad in one of the papers: Boyd Senter and His Orchestra. When the matter of Senter came up, I told Helen about this, and she called the place in the ad, and they said Senter had just closed and gone home to Mio, Michigan. She left a message with the sheriff in Mio—Senter has no phone—and Senter called back. He didn't have anything, but suggested she contact Doc Cennardo, in California, who was a drummer with Jean Goldkette, and who had a home movie with Bix Beiderbecke on it. I flipped; I'd never heard of Bix on a film. Helen reached Cennardo, and he pooh-poohed the film, saying it was a bad print, made in 1927, in Massachusetts, and that Bix was only visible for seconds. But we looked at it, and there's Bix, in a natty suit and white socks, his cornet in the side of his mouth, playing with a bunch of Goldkette musicians. All I had on Mamie Smith was a note that mentioned a 1929 short, *Jail House Blues*. Helen looked up the copyright material in the Library of Congress and discovered that Columbia Pictures had made the film. However, Columbia, it turned out, had sold TV rights to all its early shorts to a California distributor. Helen tracked down the distributor, and, miraculously, he still had a copy of the short. But there wasn't any sound track. Before sound tracks were perfected, they sometimes used regular discs that were synced with the lip movements, and when John Baker heard about the film, he said he had an acetate disc that might fit it. And, astonishingly, it did. Baker mailed the record, a twelve-incher, to Helen. When she opened the package, Lord, there it was—in six perfect pie-shaped pieces! A technician at N.B.C. stuck them back together. Then they put the record onto tape, edited out the cracked sounds—over two hundred of them —and the awful surface noise, and matched the edited tape to Mamie's lip movements, with the help of the original continuity sheets, which Columbia provided in New York. The results are fantastically clear."

Smith picked up another brownie, and I asked him how he had started his collection.

"I've been both a jazz fan and a film fan for years," he said, chewing vigorously. "But the idea of collecting jazz films only occurred to me about five years ago, when I was helping Marshall Stearns, down at the Institute of Jazz Studies, on Waverly Place. How to start? I went to Irving Klaw's old-photographs place, on Fourteenth Street, and sifted through thousands of stills dealing with all aspects of show biz. Then I read every issue of *Variety* from 1926 on up. In the early days, *Variety* had a column, 'Talking Shorts,' in which each new short was reviewed in detail. When I came to a mention of, say, a 'darkie jazz band' or 'dancers hotfooting it,' I had photostats made. I went through *Down Beat* and *Metronome*. I also went through periodicals like *Film Fun* and *Billboard*, which were even more helpful than the music magazines. I began indexing all this material, and now I have three or four thousand pages of references. I've discovered that there have been countless films made by all-Negro casts strictly for Negro audiences, and that a lot of them, terrible as they are, have jazz in them. Lena Horne was in something called *Bronze Venus* long before anyone heard of her, and Ruby Dee was in *Love and Syncopation*. I bought my first film—a Fats Waller short—three years ago, and in the last year or two I've accelerated. I spent nearly two thousand dollars last year alone on films, stills, and the like. I've begun writing a history of jazz in films, but I have so much more research to do—the Negro newspapers, the Library of Congress, the Schomberg Collection, on West 135th Street. I belong to all the film societies in New York, and every Saturday I tour all over the city, stopping at places like the Memory Shop, on Fourth Avenue, where they keep a file in my name. I look at all of the Late Late Shows on television, where things are always turning up, like *Girl Without a Room*, a Charles Ruggles picture, a while ago, in which there was a Paris night-club scene showing a Negro band dressed in Zouave uniforms. I'm positive one of the musicians was Lionel Hampton. I've been going without much sleep since I was sixteen, and it doesn't seem to bother me."

Smith told me that he was born in Los Angeles.

"My parents were on the Hungarian stage circuit that existed in this country until the depression almost knocked it out," he went on, popping a last brownie into his mouth. "In fact, my father was a kind of Hungarian Orson Welles. I didn't go to college, but I studied art in Pittsburgh and on the Coast. I joined the advertising firm of Sudler & Hennessey, where I work, in 1951. I'm an art director and a vice-president. When I first came to New York, I still wanted to paint, and I used to hang around the Cedar Street Tavern, hoping to run into De Kooning and people like that. I don't paint too much any more. This jazz-film thing has become all-consuming. I wish it could be my whole life, but that would take more bread than I'm making now from a full-time job."

The Call

IF HEAVEN does induce the final cooling of those fleshy turbines the emotions, then all great religious music, which is distinctly fleshy and highly emotional, is basically secular. (Most Protestant hymns, with their Babbitt-like rhythms and oaken melodies, *are* religious.) Indeed, some religious music shines with evil. Consider the ominous chants and down-there brass choirs in Berlioz' *Requiem*, which reverberate through the vaults not of heaven but of hell. And consider one of the newest of religious musics, the American Negro's gospel songs. Though there is probably no more aspiring religious music being composed or performed anywhere today, gospel music, which has mushroomed in the past couple of decades, is infused by its secular relative—jazz. It is largely a vocal music, whose waltzlike rhythms, simple form and harmonies, complex phrasing, and blue notes have almost all been borrowed from jazz—an odd situation, for the Negro church abhors jazz. Bessie Smith was the progenitor of Mahalia Jackson, the supreme gospel singer. Other gospel singers unmistakably echo certain jazz instrumentalists, among them Bubber Miley and Red Allen. At the same time, modern jazz has recently reached out and tapped gospel music, and is absorbing the gospel variations of jazz devices invented a generation or two ago. Gospel music is two-way in other respects. A church music, it is now enjoyed—through recordings, the radio, and concerts—by an enormous secular audience, which includes a good many whites. Its melodies (all cut from the same charming, loosely woven cloth) and its lyrics, though often banal and even lachrymose, can be majestic in the right improvisatory hands. African in origin, it celebrates a Protestant God. Its performers, a generally devout people, are given to all sorts of ejaculatory motions, frequently behaving like vaudevillians.

Most of these crosscurrents were visible at the Museum of Modern Art a week or so ago in a concert given by Marion Williams and the Stars of Faith (Frances Steadman, Catherine Parham, Henrietta Waddy, and Mattie Williams). Marion Williams, an agile, Victorian-shaped woman, was dressed in the traditional semi-bouffant Greek robes and Germanic bun of the gospel singer (she was in white, her cohorts in green), and she spent most of the evening swaying about, marching from one side of the stage to the other, clapping her hands, presenting her profile—chin stabbing heavenward, eyes shut, and hands outstretched. Her singing, equally physical, seemed an exact reflection of her movements. Each syllable was fixed to a different note, some of the notes registers apart. In fact, Miss Williams is gifted with the irrepressible ambition (but not the equipment) to slip gracefully from the coloratura range down through the contralto. (Mahalia Jackson has greater technique and less ambition.) As a result, Miss Williams' high-register statements were encased in growls or tubular moans. She sang several of the twelve selections solo, four or five with her group, which chanted contrapuntally in the background, and then allowed each of her singers a solo number. The best of these was "My Lord and I," sung by Frances Steadman, who has a camel's-hair contralto, a startling contrast to her background music, which resembled a treeful of starlings. The group's vaudeville bent reached a climax in the final number, when Miss Williams introduced her son, a two- or three-year-old got up in a blue suit and white shoes. While he executed bits and pieces of soft-shoe and the chorus rocked back and forth, Miss Williams marched off into the audience, arms up, chin reared, and singing at peak power. It was an exhilarating and even proselytizing moment, and if the chance had been offered, I would have answered the call on the spot.

The Other Cheek

LEGENDARY FIGURES are blessed properties. They enliven us by defying life and death. They are what, one morning, we hope to see in the glass. They are imaginary pied pipers forever summoning us from the crown of the next hill. Yet the best legendary figures are not legends at all; they *are* what they seem. Such is Bix Beiderbecke, the great cornetist, who died in 1931, at the age of twenty-eight. Archetypical, the Beiderbecke legend tells of a gifted small-town boy (Davenport, Iowa) who makes the big time in his early twenties, starts drinking, becomes frustrated by the chromium surroundings he must endure to make a living, drinks more heavily, loses his health, and dies, broke, of pneumonia in a baking August room in Queens. But this lugubrious chronicle, true though it is, soft-pedals the very thing that gives it backbone—Beiderbecke's extraordinary skills. For he was, unlike the majority of short-lived "geniuses," already just about complete. Had he lived, he would probably—in the manner of his close friend and peer Pee Wee Russell, who is only now reaching a serene perfection—have simply refined his playing past reproach. The adulation that encases Beiderbecke began soon after the start of his career. (Professional adulation, that is; it has been estimated that Beiderbecke was praised in print just twice during his life. Nowadays, musicians are fitted out with a full set of adjectives before making their first record.) Beiderbecke was the sort of jazz musician who provokes vigorous imitation. Andy Secrest, Sterling Bose, Leo McConville, Jimmy McPartland, Red Nichols, and Bobby Hackett were or are faithful copies, while Rex Stewart, Frankie Newton, Buck Clayton, Joe Thomas, and Roy Eldridge appear to have divided their formative years between Louis Armstrong and Beiderbecke, who also studied each other. (Why certain jazz styles are imitable and certain are not is altogether mysterious. Lester Young, Charlie Parker, and Charlie Christian have countless facsimiles, who, in turn, have *their* facsimiles. At the same time people like Thelonious Monk, Pee Wee Russell, Sidney Catlett, Billie Holiday, Vic Dickenson, and Django Reinhardt appear inimitable, and not because they are any more individualistic. But good musicians do not copy their elders. They use them only as primers—both kinds of primers. Thus, Count Basie out of Fats Waller, Dizzy Gillespie out of Roy Eldridge, and Teddy Wilson out of Earl Hines.) Despite their assiduousness, none of Beiderbecke's disciples have matched his unique *purity.* They have approximated his tone, his phrasing, and his lyricism, but his mixture of these ingredients remain secret. They've had little trouble, however, in emulating his faults, which were chiefly rhythmic. As a result, Beiderbeck's surviving followers sound disjointed and dated; he doesn't. Ample proof of this freshness is provided in a new set of reissues, "The Bix Beiderbecke Legend" (Victor), which brings together fourteen numbers (two of them alternate takes) made by Beiderbecke between 1924 and 1930 with Jean Goldkette, Paul Whiteman, Hoagy Carmichael, and a group of his own.

Beiderbecke's recordings seem almost wholly wasted. They were generally made with second-rate Dixieland bands, or with small, tightly regulated oompah groups, or with the full Goldkette or Whiteman ensemble. For the most part, the musicians involved are his inferiors. The arrangements are starchy and overdressed, and, in true neo-Gothic spirit, probably sounded dated at first playing. The rhythm sections suffer from stasis. The materials include offensive Uncle Tomming and items like "There Ain't No Sweet Man That's Worth the Salt of My Tears" and "I'll Be a Friend (with Pleasure)." Indeed, these recordings have a dumfounding insularity when one considers the contemporary output of King Oliver, Jelly Roll Morton, Fletcher Henderson, and Duke Ellington. Beiderbecke's failure to record with his peers (there are a few exceptions) was apparently due to the rigid color line that prevented mixed sessions, as well as to his own celebrated waywardness; other people generally set up his recording dates, which he simply attended. Too bad, for Beiderbecke often jammed with the great Negro musicians, and the results, reportedly, were awesome. (This last notion rings true; almost all Beiderbecke's records suggest that he was playing with his throttle only two-thirds open. The scattered exceptions emphatically prove the point.) On the other hand, the desultory groups that Beiderbecke trailed into recording studios have taken on a backhanded value. They obviously made him work. In many of his Dixieland recordings, he singlehandedly plumps the ensembles into shape, covers up for the rhythm sections, and solos brilliantly. Moreover, his accompanists set him off in an exhilarating fashion. The effeminate vocals, the fudgelike saxophones, the trick-dog muted trumpets, and the glacial drummers all point up and magnify his solos. He is the jewel in the cabbage. Some Beiderbecke aficionados hold that the ideal Beiderbecke record date would have included the likes of Frank Teschemacher, Eddie Condon, Joe Sullivan, and Gene Krupa. But what of a Beiderbecke session attended by, say, Armstrong, Jack Teagarden, Coleman Hawkins, Earl Hines, and Chick Webb?

Like all supreme stylists, Beiderbecke never bared his muscles. Not once did his uncanny tone— a carillon playing on a dry morning, an August moon over the water—go soft or sour. And it must have been close to blinding, for it shines right through the cramped, tinny recordings of the time. Beiderbecke did not *play* his notes; he struck them, as Hoagy Carmichael has pointed out. Each note hung three-dimensional in the air before being replaced by the next. He had almost no vibrato (a vibrato, in jazz, reflects either laziness or genuine emotion), and often used the whole-tone scale. Despite this affection for the hearty, all-American notes, he usually conveyed a minor, blueslike feeling. The dominant impression of Beiderbecke's work, in fact, was a paradoxical combination of the legato and the clenched, of the lackadaisical and the on-time, of calm and exuberance. In the way that winter summons up summer and summer winter, his hottest attack implied coolness, and vice versa. He might start a solo by sounding several clipped on-the-beat notes, allowing the tones from each note to wash at the next one. Then he would float into an air-current phrase and hang motionless for a second or two, like a dragonfly; abruptly start pumping again with a pattern of declamatory staccato notes, each behind the beat; slide into a brief, side-of-the-mouth run, executed with such nimbleness that it seemed made up of three or four closely related notes instead of an octave-jumping dozen; and fashion an abrupt concluding upward gliss—troops being ordered to pop to. His short solos have a teasing preview quality, while his immaculately structured long statements ("Singin' the Blues" and "I'm Coming Virginia") offer overwhelming repletion—a *compositional* repletion, at that. Primarily a melodist, Beiderbecke moved steadily toward the kind of improvisation that was later achieved by Lester Young, who also liked to linger over melodic fragments, switching them this way and that to see how much light they would catch. But Beiderbecke lacked Young's rhythmic tricks and simply pushed the beat before him, like a boy in a peanut race, or stomped directly on it. (Whenever Krupa worked behind him, Beiderbecke's rhythmic stiffness disappeared, and he gained some of the flow of his Negro colleagues.) Beiderbecke's most successful recorded solos invite immediate and unerasable committing to heart. Best of all, they have a jaunty, sun's-up quality—a declaration of fun—that is not an accident of technique. Many jazz musicians use their instruments to repay life's lumps; Beiderbecke always seemed to be turning the other cheek. Although the content of Beiderbecke's cornet work remained constant, it was increasingly overshadowed by his dabbling on the piano. Somewhere along the line, Debussy and Holst, among others, had infected him, and he began composing and playing—on piano—cloudy impressionistic pieces that he supposedly felt were his most important work. But these pieces have a sentimental, paunchy cast—despite their harmonic exploration—that uncomfortably suggest that perhaps self-pity *had* begun to set in.

The Victor set of reissues is spotty. Three of the numbers are from the Goldkette period, and are notable mainly for the long-lost "I Didn't Know," made in 1924, in which Beiderbecke plays a brief and inconclusive solo. In the other selections, he can be heard in the ensembles, beckoning the sheep after him. The seven items from Beiderbecke's Whiteman days are considerably more interesting. There are two takes of "Changes" (muted) and two of "Lonely Melody" (open-horn). Beiderbecke is gorgeous in all four, flashing out of the mire like a snowy egret. He demonstrates his hot-coolness in

The Other Cheek   161

the brisk "From Monday On," as well as in "San,"
both of them made with Whiteman splinter groups.
The last two sides, though, are invaluable. In
"Barnacle Bill the Sailor" Beiderbecke is accompanied by a curious pickup band that includes Bubber Miley (not heard), the Dorsey brothers, Benny
Goodman, Bud Freeman, Eddie Lang, and Krupa.
There is some dreadful novelty singing, but in between Beiderbecke delivers a short, furious up-
tempo explosion that reveals what he must have
sounded like in the flesh. The second record, "I'll
Be a Friend," has many of the same men and some
equally sappy singing. However, it suddenly slips
into gear when Beiderbecke appears—a derby over
his horn—for a short, superbly built solo full of
legato windings, gonglike notes, and casual harmonic
inversions. There is a new subtlety in the solo, along
with an unmistakable sense of melancholy. But this
isn't surprising, for eleven months later he was dead.

The Love Bug Will Bite You

FATS WALLER, the irrepressible pianist, organist,
composer, singer, and entertainer, who died at the
age of thirty-nine in 1943, was one of those people
who ultimately miss the mark because they are *too*
gifted. For the whole Waller, embarrassed by his
own riches into a destructive and lifelong self-
mockery, equalled less than the sum of his parts. As
a stride pianist, he masculinized the style of his
teacher, James P. Johnson, and, in turn, became
the chief inspiration of Art Tatum and Count Basie,
among others. Yet he should have been an even
better pianist; despite his rhythmic intensity, his

solos were rarely more than larking melodic embellishments. Waller has never been surpassed as a jazz organist, but the organ, empyrean and overstuffed, doesn't really fit into jazz. Had he worked harder at his composing, he might well have matched George Gershwin and Duke Ellington, the best American songwriters. Instead, he left only a tantalizing handful of great tunes—"Black and Blue," "Squeeze Me," "Ain't Misbehavin'," and "Honeysuckle Rose." Waller the singer was indistinguishable from Waller the entertainer. Almost all his vocals were expert travesties of jazz singing and of the songs themselves. Indeed, this side of Waller—clowning, scampish, and ribald—has hardened since his death into a grotesque comic mask, his epitaph, which at once conceals his other talents and grins at his final failure.

These thoughts were set in motion by a Museum of Modern Art concert given a couple of weeks ago by Dick Wellstood and the misnamed Fats Waller Alumni. Waller produced hundreds of small-band recordings, and, like most larger-than-life jazz musicians, he tended to be offhand about his choice of colleagues. But this didn't matter, for his materials were usually limited to such vacuities as "Why Do Hawaiians Sing Aloha?," "Boo Hoo," and "The Love Bug Will Bite You." And the recordings themselves were largely taken up by Waller—bounding through a chorus or so on piano, lampooning the lyrics (his eyebrows lifting and falling metronomically), rumbling encouragement behind the short solos allotted his sidemen, and shouting and thumping his way through the final ensemble. The other night, two of Waller's most durable accompanists—Gene Sedric (tenor saxophone and clarinet) and Herman Autrey (trumpet)—constituted the only Waller alumni. The rest of the group included Wellstood, on piano; Ahmed Abdul-Malik, on bass; and Panama Francis, on drums. Moreover, just one Waller-associated tune—Sedric's "Yacht Club Swing"—was offered (the six others were by Ellington, Mary Lou Williams, W. C. Handy, and Wellstood himself), and Wellstood, once a Waller disciple, now plays in a quite different style. Nonetheless, the Waller spirit—haw-hawing and big-bellied —was present during much of the evening. "C-Jam Blues," "Yacht Club Swing," a blues by Wellstood called "Tina," and Mary Lou Williams's "Lonely Moments" were genuine Wallerlike effusions (this was probably due to Sedric's and Autrey's sound; the arrangements were more complex than any that Waller used, and the solos far more extended), but perhaps the most successful number was Autrey's exquisite and distinctly un-Wallerlike "St. Louis Blues." He played the out-of-tempo first half in a muted growling fashion, and in the second half, which settled into a gentle beat, he abandoned his growl and placed his still muted horn directly beside the microphone, as if he were whispering urgently between cupped hands. Sedric was less impressive, suggesting an apprentice *castrato* in a wobbly falsetto clarinet rendition of "I Got It Bad and That Ain't Good." Abdul-Malik displayed his customary rigidity, and Francis his admiration for Sid Catlett. Wellstood, who is thirty-three, has become a kind of missing link between the most advanced swing pianist, Nat Cole, and the first bebop pianist, Bud Powell. There are flecks of everyone from Ellington to Clyde Hart in his work, but his playing —clear, thoughtful single-note figures, gangling lower-register chords, a firm, inventive left hand—is strictly his own. Waller the teacher would have liked that.

Joe Thomas

THE LAST of this season's Museum of Modern Art outdoor concerts, given by the Buster Bailey sextet, began cheerlessly. Fall was everywhere—in the escaping leaves, in the breeze, in the huddled, hooded look of the audience, which only half filled the garden. It even got into the music, a bastard Dixieland played by swing musicians who have lived long enough to see their own music go cruelly out of fashion. But the evening was saved by the performances of two of Bailey's sidemen—Vic Dickenson and the renascent Joe Thomas (the trumpeter, and no relation to the tenor saxophonist). Thomas, a short man with a broad, downcast face, is, like Bill Coleman, one of the ghosts of jazz. Now fifty-two, he has spent the past decade and more in dispirited obscurity. But, even before that, Thomas, though possessed of a consummate style, was far from renowned. During the late thirties he worked with Fletcher Henderson and Benny Carter, and in the early forties with Teddy Wilson's Café Society Uptown band. From 1941 to 1946, he made several dozen often magic small-band pickup recordings. (His 1941 sessons with Art Tatum, Edmond Hall, and Joe Turner are indelible in themselves. And in 1944 he made four sides with Roy Eldridge and Emmett Berry, plus a rhythm section; Thomas effortlessly cut his two competitors.) However, bebop and cool jazz (the quick and the dead) had arrived, and soon Thomas had vanished, along with three equally undervalued peers on his instrument—Coleman, Frankie Newton, and Doc Cheatham.

Thomas's style is an uncanny blend of Louis Armstrong, 1927, and Bix Beiderbecke, 1930, with a dash of Henry Allen, 1960. His tone, darker than Beiderbecke's, is no less marvelous. It rings, it sings, it celebrates itself. It is smooth marble and empty skies. Like all flawless-toned trumpeters, Thomas is primarily a legato performer. (His many-noted opposites, Roy Eldridge and Dizzy Gillespie, have always been short on tone; they rarely stay on one note long enough for its sound to crystallize.) He often plays in half time, loafing along near the beat or well behind it. A superb melodic embellisher, Thomas uses almost no vibrato and has an unrivaled grasp of dynamics on the trumpet. He frequently *announces* the opening notes of a phrase—this is *me*, and *these* are important notes, he seems to say —and while they are still echoing, he tucks in a short, rapid *piano* run, so that loud and soft notes sound simultaneous. The *piano* phrase is followed by another, which gives way to a second announcement, and so on. The most striking aspect of Thomas's playing is its spareness and detachment. Each solo has the perfect number of notes, as well as the perfect notes. And each, while immensely warm, gives the impression of being an aloof melodic distillation. In this sort of classicism, a muffed note is as disastrous as a slightly off-pitch glissando; indeed, one clam can sink a Thomas solo. Unfortunately, this has happened more than once in the increasingly frequent recordings that Thomas has made in the past year or so, and it happened at the Museum. Nonetheless, Thomas played with an assurance that he has not shown since the forties.

Nine of the thirteen selections were Dixieland standards. Thomas was his lucent self in "High Society," "Beale Street," "Struttin' with Some Barbecue," and "Royal Garden Blues," each of which he put definitively in its place. But his best moments occurred in a slow "Don't Blame Me." His solo, splintered notes and all, was full of calm, declaratory phrases, shaded volume changes, and that tone, which made the statues themselves glance up in surprise. Dickenson, perhaps nerved by Thomas's efforts, was memorable, mocking his way through "Tenderly" and then settling down for a lyrical and straight—well, almost straight—version of "Basin Street" that was knotted together with a couple of spectacular breaks. Buster Bailey has long been a puzzle. Though he is technically as gifted as such contemporaries as Benny Goodman and Artie Shaw, his work has never seemed more than a flow of handsome arabesques, and in recent years this lack of content has been emphasized by pitch difficulties. The rest of the group—Red Richards, piano; Leonard Gaskin, bass; and Jackie Williams, drums—were steady. May Thomas's new career be as constant.

Abstract

FOLK MUSIC, like Spode china and Hitchcock chairs, is a practical art. The great body of European balladry both carried and ornamented the news. The American blues chronicle the sorrows of the Negro. The Indian *ragas* (the most refined and complex of all folk musics) celebrate certain seasons or times of day. Until the mid-forties, jazz, which since then has more or less been forced into the fine arts, was primarily a dance music. However, there's a winsome notion, which can be neither proved nor disproved, that it was also, and is, a handy reflector of its times. New Orleans and Chicago jazz embody the cheerful ingenuousness of the First World War and the twenties. The post-depression era can be found in miniature in the bureaucratic big bands of the late thirties. (Only the blues had the stamina to record the depression.) Bebop—lyric, nervous, *furioso*—symbolizes the Second World War, while its first cousin, cool jazz, mirrors the fake euphoria that set in soon after. The newest revolution in jazz—the music of Ornette Coleman, Cecil Taylor, Charlie Mingus, and George Russell—is uncannily topical. A largely free atonal music, it eerily reflects the mad, undecided temper of the present. This is clear in two momentous new recordings—"The World of Cecil Taylor" (Candid) and "Free Jazz: A Collective Improvisation by the Ornette Coleman Double Quartet" (Atlantic). Despite their occasional shortcomings, these recordings indicate the direction in which jazz is to go.

"The World of Cecil Taylor" is the best of the handful of utopian records that Taylor has made. It also displays a considerable advance over his first recording, a revolutionary effort set down in 1957. Taylor occupies an odd place in jazz. Leagues ahead of most of his contemporaries, he has, unlike the customary prophet, no followers, even distant ones. At the same time, he is roughly neck and neck with Coleman, Don Ellis, Mingus, Eric Dolphy, and Russell. He is, in short, an accidental co-leader of the first great upheaval in jazz since the arrival, in the early forties, of Charlie Parker, Dizzy Gillespie, and Thelonious Monk. This movement is still nameless. It has inaccurately been called "third-stream" music. It has also been termed "space music," and, with a sigh of desperation, "the new thing." Since this music is highly abstract, why not "abstract jazz"? Anyway, abstract jazz is as far removed from bebop as bebop is from swing. An attempt to free jazz of the arbitrary rules and regulations hit upon in its earliest days (and adhered to even by bebop musicians), it sets aside tonality, the unwavering beat, the conventional chorus structure, and improvisation that is based chiefly on chord progressions. Discarded shackles are invariably replaced by new, if at first invisible, ones, and in abstract jazz these paradoxically take the form of absolute freedom. Every conceivable rhythm is used, and the tempos may be halved, doubled, tripled, or slowly accelerated or decelerated. Sometimes, in cadenza fashion, there isn't any beat at all. (The soloists in one number of a recent recording by Don Ellis simply chose their own tempos.) Improvisation is often built around a brief motif, an arbitrary row of notes, or the twelve-tone scale. Or it may be wholly free and off the top of the head. The solists' melodic lines (usually not melodic at all) tend to be extremely long, altogether ignoring bar divisions and the standard chorus measure. The new musicians are also experimenting tonally with a variety of emanations that fall between anguished human and electronic sounds. Yet for all these neoteric methods, abstract jazz is not aimless and amoebic. The lyricism of the blues colors it, the tension-and-release patterns of older jazz are its skeleton, and it possesses the unified non-unity of all abstract art. Most important, it challenges—almost for the first time in jazz—the emotions *and* the intellect.

In 1957, Taylor's work approximated what might have happened if a gifted modern classical pianist had sat down at the keyboard and attempted to improvise whole compositions in the combined manners of Debussy, Stravinsky, and Bartók. Though this music was worked out against jazz rhythms, it rarely stated the beat, and its largely atonal substance seemed foreign, and even inimical, to jazz. Dense, dark, and rather desperate, it offered an on-the-spot survey of contemporary classical music. Since then, Taylor has begun to digest his classical training (four years at the New England Conservatory) and turn more firmly toward jazz. His playing now has breathing room, and is ten or twenty pounds lighter. Its buttonholing urgency is often transmuted into a subtle but unmistakable lyricism; some of Taylor's chords are even unabashedly blueslike. (Like all great rebels, Taylor has sniffed at the past before moving on, for his work also demonstrates a knowledge of ragtime, boogie-woogie, and stride piano.) Moreover, his present approach, as opposed to his shapeless earlier one, is a visionary attempt to fashion *each number* into an indivisible whole, just as older jazz musicians constructed an indivisible *chorus.* Taylor uses every sort of device to achieve this enlarged structure. He rarely plays in a tempo; he implies one, he nods at it, he rides slightly to one side of it. For minutes at a time, he may invent bitter, unbroken series of single right-hand notes, which fall like acid on powerful, irregular chaconnes in the left hand. He may then slightly increase his volume and play a formidable two-handed tremolo, and, lowering his voice again, issue shocking, painful dissonances, which may give way to a resounding rest and then impeccably struck chords that leap through most of the registers on the keyboard. (Taylor's technique is stunning.) Non-climactic music is flat-footed, and Taylor knows this. Each of his numbers is a true orchestral composition pivoted on one or more climaxes, which may occur at the end, in the middle, or even at the start. Indeed, his work makes Art Tatum's greatest pyramids appear hollow. Taylor is never euphoric. Each step of the way is an equal mixture of passion and thought, which, in catharsis fashion, is virtually *forced* on the listener —an exhilarating if bone-trying experience.

There are five pieces in Taylor's new recording. Three are his and two are standards. He is accompanied by a couple of holdovers from his first record —Buell Neidlinger, bass, and Dennis Charles, drums. Also present for two numbers is Archie Shepp, on tenor saxophone. Taylor has used horn players before, in recordings and in the flesh, and the results have been uneasy. Like Tatum, Taylor swallows them. Ornette Coleman has unconsciously come closest to Taylor's orchestral approach, but the two have played together just once, and briefly at that. Perhaps the only way for predominantly single-voiced instruments to match Taylor is through the kind of ensemble combinations invented by Coleman, Mingus, and George Russell. Be that as it may, Shepp is surprisingly successful. The most fascinating number on the record is an unearthly rendition by Taylor—with rhythm section only— of Richard Rodgers's "This Nearly Was Mine." Ten minutes long, it is, aside from a few ominous discords, an ephemeral series of blues-derived variations —done first arhythmically and then with a beat— in which the melody keeps rising into view just beneath the surface and then falling away. (For a long time, Taylor considered even an indirect statement of the melody heretical.) The number swells and subsides, swells and subsides, and the lovely, inexhaustible single-note passages practically lilt, while the chordal sections are full of blue notes and Monkish dissonances. It is the sort of rare jazz performance that is constructed in layers, each more delicate and finely tempered than the last. "Lazy Afternoon," four minutes longer, is another standard, with much of the same quality, which is intensified by Shepp's two anthracite-toned solos. The number reaches a distinct climax in the middle and then gradually melts away through a long and intricately textured duologue between Taylor and Shepp. "Air," "E.B.," and "Port of Call" are more typical up-tempo excursions, full of atonal explosions, bits of ragtime, ice-breaking dissonances, and racking tensions.

An appreciable part of the success of the record is due to Charles's support. Most drummers these days either obstruct the proceedings or wander off by themselves. But Charles creates a steady, listening foundation for Taylor, whether Taylor chooses to use it or not. He even predicts some of Taylor's moves. In "E.B." he underscores perfectly a couple of Taylor phrases with the snare and bass drum, although there is no indication that Taylor is going to play those particular phrases. And at the end of "Air" there is a marvelous exchange of breaks between the two; Taylor improvises on Charles's patterns, which, in turn, are enlarged upon by Charles, and so on. Neidlinger is one of the handful of skilled young bassists who have appeared in the past several years, and he plays with a sympathy and inventiveness that seem to radiate Taylor's work.

Ornette Coleman is working toward the same goal as Taylor but from the opposite quarter. Taylor is a well-schooled classical pianist whose use of atonality and free improvisation is conscious and academic; Coleman is a self-taught musician whose methods are mostly intuitive. In fact, Coleman considers such devices as the thirty-two-bar chorus, the old-fashioned beat, and chord-based improvisation artificial. He does not merely improvise on a tune, he improvises on what he regards as its *essence*—rhythmic, melodic, tonal, or lyric. He writes most of his materials (they begin roughly where Thelonious Monk's stop), and, putting the cart before the horse, designs each number to provoke a specific attack. Some of Coleman's works are pure rhythmic exercises, constructed of many-noted figures that move rapidly up and down the scale. In performance, Coleman may handle one of these by exaggerating its rhythmic structure, by playing it backward, by distilling it within a single phrase, or by pressing the entire composition into a rhythmless legato statement. Other Coleman numbers consist of long, graceful melodic lines based on the blues. He will rummage mercilessly through the emotions inherent in such numbers, so that we get a lament on loneliness or racial injustice or plain Sunday melancholy. Still other Coleman compositions are hinged on tonal aberrations or peculiarities of pitch, which he investigates—no matter how unearthly the sounds—to *their* limits. In short, Coleman thinks of a number not as a melody sewn to a set of chords but as a specific musical state of mind. At first hearing, he sounds inflexible, crude, and even brutish. His tone appears thick-thumbed and heavy. He plays insane and seemingly purposeless runs. His intensity is apoplectic. But once Coleman's ground rules have been absorbed, the strange timbres and dervish rhythms become less imperious and even tend to point up the blueslike passages and snatches of often beautiful melody that occur more frequently than one had first thought. Most important, Coleman's work is bound tightly together by a passion associated more with the Romantic composers than with jazz. However, his music is not Lisztian; rather, it falls in that zone where compassion is levelheaded and sound of heart.

Unlike the great prima donnas of swing and bebop, who are basically soloists, Coleman belongs with Mingus, John Lewis, Jimmy Giuffre, and George Russell, all of whom place equal emphasis on collective interplay and soloing. As a result, Coleman has made his various quartets (himself, a trumpeter, a bassist, and a drummer) into seamless units that nonetheless sport an individual daring comparable to that of most Mingus groups. His dissonant "unison" ensemble figures are treated with aplomb, and during the solos the accompanists simultaneously counterpoise and interpret what the soloist does. Coleman's new recording is an attempt to magnify these achievements. Its instrumentation includes two trumpeters (Don Cherry and Freddie Hubbard), two reeds (Coleman and Eric Dolphy on bass clarinet), two bassists (Charlie Haden and the late Scott LaFaro), and two drummers (Billy Higgins and Eddie Blackwell). Moreover, it consists entirely of a single, unbroken free improvisation (no key, no chords, no theme, no time limits) that lasts just over thirty-six minutes. The result, the longest jazz recording ever made, is astonishing. Like Cecil Taylor's improvisations the number is an unbroken whole, and it goes like this: brief introductory ensemble; Dolphy's solo (five minutes); ensemble; Hubbard (five minutes); ensemble; Coleman (ten minutes); ensemble; Cherry (five minutes); ensemble; Haden (two and a half minutes); ensemble; LaFaro (two and a half minutes);

ensemble; Blackwell (two and a half minutes); ensemble; Higgins (two and a half minutes); closing ensemble. The tempo is roughly medium—roughly because Blackwell and Higgins, who, like the bassists, play together throughout, do not keep a level four-four beat but revolve arbitrarily around a kind of rolling, overlapping de-dat-de-dat-de-dat-de-dat shuffle rhythm. The only written parts of the number are the ensembles, which vary from typical Coleman patterns to short bursts. But there are other collective passages. During the solos, the remaining horns occasionally move in behind for group improvisations that may increase in intensity and volume until the soloist becomes totally enmeshed, or that may simply reach a loud mutter and fade away, returning the soloist to the rhythm section. These marvelous collective outbursts operate both as helpmeets for the faltering (Cherry is the only one who gets into difficulty, and the resulting assistance is so warm it almost sends him under for good) and as celebrations (these occur half a dozen times during Coleman's memorable statement) for the superior. They also go directly back to King Oliver's Creole Jazz Band, and in places they even bear a nightmarish resemblance to the neolithic brass-band recordings made in Alabama in the fifties by Frederic Ramsey.

The contour of the "Improvisation," though largely accidental, is just about right. The first ensemble opens with an avalanche of staccato scales, which are quickly ironed out into a soaring legato figure, which, in turn, is followed by Dolphy's solo. Dolphy maintains this uplands feeling remarkably well; Hubbard, pretending here and there that he is Miles Davis, dissipates it somewhat; and Coleman gradually and casually brings it to the highest point on the record. Cherry follows, rather fumblingly, and the elevation slowly decreases through the bass and drum solos before being momentarily heightened in the brief final ensemble. (A longer and more complex closing ensemble, which might have been improvised rather than written, would have tied the entire number together more satisfactorily; its present ending has a disquieting midair quality.) Coleman's solo is by far the best he has recorded. Barring a few dicty arpeggios and "Night on Bald Mountain" screeches, it is mainly a series of blues phrases, some of them reminiscent of the plow-and-mule alto-saxophone playing you used to hear in the thirties on "city" blues records. These phrases disarmingly develop an emotional momentum that becomes nearly unbearable by the time the releasing connective ensemble comes along. But the bassists come close to Coleman, and together attain remarkable lyricism. (LaFaro, a brilliant bassist, was killed in an automobile accident last spring, at the age of twenty-five. His solo, and Haden's, are perfect epitaphs.) Haden begins with half-time single notes (LaFaro runs up and down in the high register behind him), to which he adds a sitarlike vibrato. He pauses, and, strumming his instrument like a guitar, shifts into flowing tremolo chords (the drummers hustle into a kind of oblique double time, with brushes on their snares), which gradually separate until the chords fall on the beat, behind the beat, and finally are barely sounded, while LaFaro and the drummers imperceptibly allow *their* lines to dissolve. An abrupt ensemble discord restores order, and LaFaro opens his solo with high, rapid single notes (Haden plays harplike figures behind), which are slowly transposed into beautiful flamenco chords. A poignant

Django Reinhardt single-note passage follows (Haden is now in a straight four-four beat, and the contrast is stunning), culminating in fast, ascending runs that are so explicit they take your breath away. The drummers' solos (each man backs the other) are almost as good, and Higgins is particularly impressive in a statement made up wholly of rising and falling cymbal splashes dotted with snare offbeats.

"Improvisation" causes earache the first time through, especially for those new to Coleman's music. The second time, its cacophony lessens and its complex balances and counter-balances begin to take effect. The third time, layer upon layer of pleasing configurations—rhythmic, melodic, contrapuntal, tonal—becomes visible. The fourth or fifth listening, one swims readily along, about ten feet down, breathing the music like air.

Sabbatical

WHEN LIFE becomes nothing but a bowl of clichés, how many young and successful people of non-independent means have the resilience and backbone to withdraw completely from the world and reorganize, refuel, retool, and refurbish themselves? Well, there is *one* such heroic monk—Sonny Rollins, the thirty-one-year-old tenor saxophonist. In the summer of 1959, Rollins, finding himself trapped between burgeoning success and burgeoning displeasure with his playing, dropped abruptly and voluntarily into oblivion, where he remained until recently, when he momentously reappeared at the Jazz Gallery, with a quartet. At the time of his self-banishment, Rollins was, among other things, the most influential practitioner on his instrument to come along since Lester Young and Coleman Hawkins; the unofficial head of the hard-bop school (a refinement of bebop); and one of the first of the now plentiful semi-abstract jazz improvisers. As a result, his Return—rumored for months —took on a kind of millennial air, which I got caught up in several days before the event by having a chat with the Master himself. A tall, broad-shouldered, thin-waisted man who resembles a genie, Rollins has a shaved head, a long, lemon-shaped face, slightly Oriental eyes, a generous nose, and a full, non-pointed goatee. He was wearing, from the skin outward, a gray turtleneck sweater, a blue-and-white-striped button-down shirt, open at the neck, and a handsome blue-gray V-neck sweater, above gray slacks. This ensemble was rounded out with shined black space shoes, a black porkpie hat with a medium brim, and a gabardine overcoat.

I asked Rollins why he had decided to retire and whether his sabbatical had been a success. "People are not doing things as well as they can do them any more," he replied. "The par of products is not high enough, and in 1959 I felt that way about my playing. The extraneous things had gotten in the way of it. I didn't have time to practice, and I wanted to study more. I was playing before more and more people, and not being able to do my best. There was no doubt that I had to leave the scene, and it was just a matter of when I could bring it about. I'd lost the ability to play what I *wanted* to play every night without the interference of emotionalism. I was filled with question marks. Also, as a leader, you have to keep the audience.

You have to think about those people, and you have to fill the image the critics make of you. At the same time, you have to maintain your product. There is an almost invisible line there. But I'm no longer nervous about those things. I don't read the critics any more. Something I want to know, I go and ask a musician I respect. I'm bringing a whole new understanding to the scene. If no one comes to the opening, if they don't like me, if they rush out—I'm prepared for all those contingencies, and they would not influence me adversely."

Rollins looked at a white handkerchief he was holding in his right hand. "I've been practicing and practicing," he continued. "When I quit working, I tried to revise the way I played the horn. Completely. But then I amended that. Instead, I have made an exploration of the horn. I practiced at home all day at first, but I was conscious of bothering people. There's a law that allows me to play from seven to eleven, if I don't overdo it. But I was very loud. There was a girl next door who was having a baby, and I was anxious to see if my playing would give that baby bad ears. I was anxious to see how it would be born, what effect my playing would have. But it turned out a very beautiful child. You go near it, it laughs. It listens. Then I discovered the Williamsburg Bridge, which is near where I live, and I stopped practicing at home. I started walking over the bridge, and I found it's a superb place to practice. Night or day. You're up over the whole world. You can look down on the whole scene. There is the skyline, the water, the harbor. It's a beautiful scene, a panoramic scene. The bridge offers certain advantages that can't be duplicated indoors. You can blow as loud as you want. It makes you think. The grandeur gives you perspective.

And people never bother you. I saw the same people almost every day. Sometimes they stopped and listened, sometimes they just went by. New Yorkers are very sophisticated. When I wasn't on the bridge, I studied piano, harmony, and counterpoint with Max Hughes, who's from Frisco. I've also tried to improve my health. I've quit smoking. Every now and then I goof off for short periods, but by and large I've licked the habit. I've cut down on drinking, and I lift bar bells every day. I walk and walk. I have to have good lungs and quick fingers. The whole country needs exercise, and I feel if I keep in shape other people will see me and they'll do it. My wife and I have gotten along all right. We have a very modest apartment, and she's been working, and I've received royalties from records and tunes. I even taught a little at the end—after I got to where the question marks stopped."

Rollins wrapped the handkerchief tightly around his right hand. "I was born right here, and I was forced to take piano lessons at eight, or around there. I didn't like it. But I had a musical ear, and I used to hear my brother practicing violin. And my sister played the piano. Later on, a friend of mine who had a tenor sax had his picture taken with it. It all looked so nice. It inspired me to get a horn—an alto. I listened to Louis Jordan a lot. I mean he gassed me. He had the first of the little blues bands, like what Ray Charles has now. Coleman Hawkins influenced me after that, and I started playing the alto like a tenor, using a tenor reed. Then I switched to tenor, and people said I sounded like an alto. I started jobbing around, and made my first records in 1948. I worked with Charlie Parker—he solidified things, the linear approach and the chord approach—and later with

Max Roach and my own groups. My new group will have Jim Hall on guitar. I want to do more things with harmony, and he'll give me the framework. He's an excellent soloist. But it's most important he's willing to do things for the good of the group. He has an attitude to work *for* the group. I'll also have Bob Cranshaw, who's very, very good, on bass, and Walter Perkins on drums."

Rollins stood up, folded his handkerchief carefully, put it in his pocket, and shook hands with me. "I've got to walk my dog, and then we practice at two o'clock. I'll miss the bridge, but I've got to begin to get this group tight."

Rollins's opening at the Jazz Gallery made it clear that the only differences between the old Sonny Rollins and the new one are that he is even better now and that he suddenly sounds—and this isn't meant pejoratively—rather old-fashioned. The self-criticism that led to Rollins's sabbatical without pay was pretty rarefied, for his playing appeared, if anything, to be steadily improving. His once mannered and querulous tone had become larger and freer, his singular thematic-rhythmic approach to improvisation was a constantly changing delight, and he had perfected an awesome authoritativeness that permitted him to hypnotically play entire numbers *a cappella*. These virtues have simply been intensified in the renascent Rollins. His playing, edged with even more wit and sarcasm, has become almost unbearably *personal*. This is not to say that Rollins, in the sentimental catch phrase, "tells his story" through his horn. Instead, he creates sounds that mirror precisely his formidable personality and that are played in such a way as to be well-nigh evangelistically stamped on the listener. Whether one is willing or not, one becomes Rollins's follower each time he picks up his horn. Rollins's new, seeming old-fashionedness is not his doing. During his absence, Ornette Coleman and Eric Dolphy arrived with an attack that goes a step or two beyond Rollins's semi-abstract one. Rollins, however, understands Coleman and Dolphy thoroughly (he once played early-morning duets with Dolphy on a Pacific beach), and perhaps in time he will beat them at their own game—if, that is, he decides it is worth playing at all.

Rollins's tone, though ballroom-size, is hard when compared to that of Chu Berry, Ben Webster, or Coleman Hawkins. But it is the hardness of muscle, not stone—a warm hardness. Like those of Ornette Coleman and Cecil Taylor, Rollins's solos, free of the rule-sticks of measures and choruses, are in each case an attempt to fashion an indivisible composition. They are also free of dependence on chord structures and ordinary four-four time. Rollins, however, is kinder to his listeners than Coleman and Taylor. In the course of a solo, he will return repeatedly to the theme or rhythmic motif on which it is based, placing signposts in the snows of his variations. But he is never straightforward. Frequently, the theme he improvises on is itself a variation on the original melody, and whenever he goes back to this theme he varies it still further, though always leaving it recognizable. As he delights, he teaches. Rollins's favorite materials are usually standards done in medium tempos. He will play one chorus of the melody, and the amount of pressure he applies to it may depend on his attitude toward the tune or toward life in general. If the world appears askew or the tune in need of improvement, Rollins will slyly and sardonically slur certain phrases, end others with abominating smears, and inject ridiculing rhythms. Frumpy melodies are made frumpier, slick ones are shattered, and good ones are strained to the joists. After this introductory chorus, which forces the listener to hear the original melody in a curiously objective way, he will invent a short variation on it and devote several choruses to taking this variation painstakingly apart, rebuilding it, taking it apart again, rebuilding it differently, and so forth. Often he will do this with series of single notes separated by speaking silences and suspended in an almost rhythmless void. He will sound some notes experimentally, barely touching them, hold others expressionlessly for several measures (Rollins's vibrato is sparing), and cut the rest off abruptly. Here and there, he will stir in fast, urgent runs. Or he may play whole swatches of the melody, stretching them, contracting them, and turning them over and over in whatever inner winds possess him. All this is done with unflagging wit, with the parodist's sense of corrective admiration. At the same time, Rollins's personality dominates the musical aspects of these displays, filling each note or fragment or phrase with a distinctive, almost moral flavor. Rollins, in short, is the true stylist—form and content handsomely locked in each other's embrace.

Last week, Rollins gave the second "Jazz Profiles" concert of the season at the Museum of Modern Art. His group consisted of Jim Hall, Bob Cranshaw (bass), and Albert Heath (drums), and the program, not unexpectedly, included five standards and two Rollins originals, one a blues. For the first half of the concert, something—worries, the weather, the surroundings—was too much with Rollins, and he sounded strained and apprehensive.

The tempos themselves were indicative. "Oleo" and "Will You Still Be Mine" were recklessly fast, and Rollins largely slid over them, using more notes than there was space for, and never allowing any of them to settle to the bottom of the listener's mind. There were exceptions in the medium-tempo "Gone with the Wind," which Rollins opened with a long and marvelous ad-lib passage and closed with a parody of one of those swelling, periwigged Coleman Hawkins codas. And in a slow "Sentimental Mood" he bent Ellington's melody affectionately out of shape, using low, nearly derisive notes and lemony smears. But it was an unsettling hour or so; the dampers were shut, the lights too bright.

Knute Rockne must have been backstage during intermission, because the second half of the evening was exultant. The first number, "Love Letters," was taken at a medium-slow tempo, and had a classic, mocking first chorus by Rollins, who, through exaggeratedly legato half-time phrases and heavy choke-toned notes, seemed to drag the melody out of its very shell. His solo was full of double-stops and breathless figures that moved from the highest register to the lowest. "I'm Old-Fashioned" was given over to Hall, and then the group played a twenty-minute fast blues, "Sonnymoon." After a brief ensemble riff, Rollins arranged a sparse, severe tableau of notes, allowed these to gradually multiply and grow swaggering (Rollins paying his particular brand of respects to Hawkins, Lester Young, and Charlie Parker), and then passed into chorus after chorus of semi-atonal passages, possibly aimed at Ornette Coleman. He must have put together thirty choruses, each of them different, startling, and funny. Hall, whose background chords were brilliant, followed manfully, and the piece ended with

Dinosaurs in the Morning   184

a brisk round of four-bar exchanges. Once a placid, timid, and somewhat academic guitarist, Hall has perfected his rhythmic and harmonic sense, and, unlike his contemporaries, he never glosses over his notes. Two-thirds of his solos were good, and the rest exceptional. Cranshaw is a Wilbur Ware student, and Heath an attentive, if nervous, drummer. Rollins isn't merely back; he is looming.

The How-Long Blues

WRITING CRITICALLY about aging institutions is like trying to review a mountain: No matter what you say, nothing changes. This long-suffering thought has been caused by a concert given last week by Duke Ellington at Town Hall, at which the Master served the same cold creamed chicken, mashed potatoes, and peas that he has been offering in concerts and night clubs during most of the past decade. The Ellington institution is made up, of course, of two interdependent parts. The first consists of El- lington and Billy Strayhorn, a mysterious and inex- tricably entwined composing-arranging team, which has produced, singly and together, many of the in- eradicable American melodies and compositions of the past thirty years. The second part is the El- lington band. (Ellington's piano playing is the de- lightful fretwork that adorns this structure.) Nei- ther part of this entente does very well without the other. A lot of Ellington's and Strayhorn's best songs and concertos have been written around the stylistic perfections and oddities of specific Elling- ton soloists. At the same time, these soloists have often flowered under—and sometimes been spoiled by—this admiration. As a result, Ellington's and Strayhorn's most successful efforts were fired by the singular 1940-42 aggregation, which included Cootie Williams, Rex Stewart, Tricky Sam Nanton, Ben Webster, Johnny Hodges, Lawrence Brown, Harry Carney, Jimmy Blanton, and Sonny Greer, and which, in turn, was fired by Ellington and Strayhorn, and so forth. (Brown, Carney, and Hodges are still with Ellington, but Brown and Hodges have taken extended sabbaticals at various times.) These men had been trained by Ellington and had trained *him* for well over a decade, and when, in the late forties, they died or drifted away, to be inexplicably replaced by inferiors, an inevitable creative vacuum set in. To be sure, Ellington and Strayhorn still write a great deal, and the present band frequently sounds, largely because of Hodges, Brown, and Carney, much as it did twenty years ago. But this is not nearly enough when one considers the unmatched musical records that Ellington has set. Ellington's present work, though often fragmentary or windy, maddeningly suggests that his talents are *not* diminished, and, concomitantly, there are dozens of eminently qualified free-lance musicians around (Ellington alumni included), who spend regrettable amounts of time looking for work.

Here, as it was set forth at Town Hall, is Ellington's present all-purpose program. The twenty-odd numbers included two sets of medleys (three selections in the first, ten in the second) of Ellington tunes, mostly old; three peremptory selections from recent scores done by Ellington for television and the movies; an un-Ellingtonish "Stompin' at the Savoy"; six sketchy solo numbers for Jimmy Hamilton, Cat Anderson, Sam Woodyard, and Hodges;

"Diminuendo and Crescendo in Blue"; three vocals by a singer with a leaden bass voice; and four vocals by Lonnie Johnson, the venerable and not particularly distinguished blues singer and guitarist, who recorded with Ellington in 1928. The law of averages forced good things to happen. Hodges, particularly in "All of Me" and "The Sunny Side of the Street," was first-rate, and so, in half a dozen numbers, were Brown (open horn and plunger muted) and the ineluctable Harry Carney. Johnson pitted against the band was refreshingly freakish—the country mouse and the town mouse exchanging saws and epigrams—and the contest produced one memorable, if irrelevant, instant: a lovely blues trumpet obbligato by Howard McGhee, a fine and recently resurrected bebop musician who, however, was not heard from again during the evening. And, finally, there were those celebrated textures and voicings, which, no matter how sloppily executed, amount to a series of timbres and harmonies unique in music. But to hear these things one had to suffer through a drum solo by Woodyard, who gets a sound from his instrument that suggests pease porridge in the pot, nine days old; equally faceless solos by Anderson, Russell Procope, Paul Gonsalves, Aaron Bell, and Hamilton, the last of whom belongs not in a jazz band but on the staff of a music school; a generally Philistine mien among the musicians; and a choice of materials that totally obscured the fact that Ellington has a priceless store of pieces that either have not been played in decades or have never been played at all. Ellington's unfailingly regal and articulate presence was reminiscent, as it has been for years, of a defeated commanding general who has just surrendered his sword but expects it to be returned forthwith.

The How-Long Blues

Cheers for Red Allen

THE PRE-EMINENCE of Louis Armstrong from 1925 to 1935 had one unfortunate effect: it tended to blot out the originality and skill of several contemporary trumpeters who, though they listened to Armstrong, had pretty much gone their own way by 1930. These included, among others, Bobby Stark, Joe Smith, Jabbo Smith (no relation), Bill Coleman, and Henry (Red) Allen. Stark and Joe Smith are dead. Jabbo Smith, a scarifying musician, lives in Milwaukee and performs rarely. Coleman, in Europe, still displays much of his grace. But Allen, the most steadfast of the three, and a distinct influence on Roy Eldridge, who taught Dizzy Gillespie, who taught Miles Davis, and so forth, is playing (usually in New York) with more subtlety and warmth than at any other time in his career. This is abundantly evident in two fairly recent and rather odd releases, "Red Allen Meets Kid Ory" and "We've Got Rhythm: Kid Ory and Red Allen" (Verve), in which Allen, lumped with second- and third-class musicians, plays with a beauty and a let's-get-this-on-the-road obstinacy that transform both records into superior material.

A tall, comfortably oval-shaped man of fifty-four, with a deceptively sad basset-hound face, Allen, born in Algiers, Louisiana, has had a spirited career, despite the shadows he has been forced to work in. He played briefly with King Oliver in 1927, and two years later he joined Luis Russell, another Oliver alumnus. Russell's band was possibly the neatest, hottest, and most imaginative group of its time. It was also, thanks to Russell's arrangements and rhythmic innovations and to Allen's already exploratory solos, a considerably advanced one. In 1933, Allen joined Fletcher Henderson, with whom he continued his avant-garde ways, and after a period with the Blue Rhythm Band he came face to face in 1937 with Goliath himself when he became a practically silent member of Louis Armstrong's you-go-your-way, I'll-go-mine big band, a group kept afloat by Sid Catlett, J. C. Higginbotham, Charlie Holmes, and the leader. Since 1940, Allen has led a succession of often excellent small groups, which have included Higginbotham, Edmond Hall, Don Stovall (alto saxophone), and Alvin Burroughs. Allen's recording activity has been prolific; he was particularly active during the thirties, when he set down fifty or sixty numbers with small groups, some of which were unabashed attempts to make money ("The Miller's Daughter Marianne," "The Merry-Go-Round Broke Down," "When My Dream Boat Comes Home") and some of which were, and are, first-rate jazz records ("Why Don't You Practice What You Preach," "There's a House in Harlem for Sale," "Rug Cutter's Swing," "Body and Soul," and "Rosetta"). Lamentably, only two or three of these, along with two classic sides made in 1939 with Lionel Hampton, are now available.

Allen's style had just about set by the time he joined Russell. There were traces in it of Oliver and Armstrong, but more apparent were its careless tone, its agility, and a startling tendency to use unprecedentedly long legato phrases and strange notes and chords that jazz musicians hadn't, for the most part, had the technique or courage to use before. Allen's playing also revealed an emotion and a partiality to the blues that often seemed to convert every-thing he touched into the blues. But his adventur-ousness and technique weren't always in balance; he hit bad notes, he blared, and he was ostenta-tious. Once in a while he would start a solo com-mandingly and then, his mind presumably going blank, would suddenly falter, ending his statement in a totally different mood and tenor, as if he were attempting to glue parts of two unmatchable solos together. By the mid-forties, Allen's work had, in fact, turned increasingly hard and showy—he flut-tered his valves, used meaningless runs, and affected a stony tone—and this peculiar shrillness continued into the fifties. Then, six or so years ago, Allen made a pickup recording with Tony Parenti, the clarinet-ist, for Jazztone, and, not long after, one for Victor with Higginbotham, Coleman Hawkins, and Cozy Cole, and a remarkable new Allen broke into view. Perhaps sheer middle-aged physical wear—a reluc-tance to *blow* so hard, a reluctance to try and *prove* so much—was the reason. Or perhaps he had been listening to younger and milder trumpeters like Miles Davis and Art Farmer. For his tone has be-come softer and fuller, he shies away from the upper register (he spends a good deal of time inflating sumptuous balloons in the lowest register), his cus-tomarily long figures are even longer, his sensuous, mid-thirties affection for the blues has again become dominant, and he often employs harmonies that would please Thelonious Monk. In short, he gives the impression not of hammering at his materials from the outside but, in the manner of Lester Young and Pee Wee Russell, of transforming them insist-ently if imperceptibly from the inside, like a mole working just under the grass. The results, particu-larly in slower tempos (the old shrillness sometimes recurs at faster speeds), can be unbelievably stirring. An Allen solo in a slow blues may go like this: He will start with a broad, quiet, shushing note, pause, repeat the note, and, using almost no vibrato, fasten two more notes onto it, one slightly higher and one slightly lower, pause again (Allen's frequent use of silences is another new aspect of his work, as is his more expert use of dynamics), repeat and enlarge the second phrase a little way down the scale, and, without a rest, get off a legato phrase, with big intervals, that may shatter into a rapid run and then be reformed into a dissonant blue note, which he will delightfully hold several beats longer than one expects; he then finishes this with a full vibrato and tumbles into a quick, low, almost under-the-breath flourish of half a dozen notes. Such a solo bears constant re-examination; it is restless, oblique, surprising, lyrical, and demanding. It seizes the listener's emotions, recharges them, and sends them fortified on their way.

The pairing of Allen with the venerable Kid Ory is curious, to say the least. Allen is a modernish swing musician, and Ory is one of the last representatives of genuine New Orleans style. His solos are gruff paraphrases of the melody, while Allen's are intricate temples of sound. Moreover, Allen's leisurely, independent melodic lines are far too spacious to fit within the limitations of the New Orleans ensemble. But perhaps all this is to the good. Ory's sandpaper tone and elementary patterns tend to set off Allen's housetop-to-housetop swoops, and since Allen can't, or won't, adapt himself to the ensemble, he simply solos throughout most of the recordings, which gives us twice as much of him. By and large, the first of the Verve records is the better. Of the seven numbers, all standards, three—

"Blues for Jimmy," "Ain't Misbehavin'," and "Tishomingo Blues"—present Allen at his peak. In fact, his single-chorus solo in the slow "Blues for Jimmy" is faultless. This is nearly true of his work on the Waller tune, which is full of blue notes and wind-borne figures. (Puzzlingly, neither of the two vocals is by Allen, who, in addition to his other merits, is one of the handful of true jazz singers. His voice is in between Armstrong's and Jelly Roll Morton's, and because of its almost feline, back-of-the-beat phrasing it has long foretold his playing of today.) The second session contains seven more standards, which are notable for Allen's playing in "Some of These Days," in which he tries a few teetering but generally successful auld-lang-syne upper-register handstands; for, in "Christopher Columbus," his muted chorus, which is followed by an open-horn one that begins in his lowest, or trombone, register; and for his three remarkably sustained choruses in the medium-tempo "Lazy River." The rest of the band stands around and watches, so to speak, and only the drummer, Alton Redd, gets in the way.

Part Four: 1962

bear almost no resemblance to their original form. Some have been expanded, many more have been endlessly refined and polished. Others, not up to such pressure, have been replaced by new and often superior material. But this admirable compositional and improvisational elasticity may not save the group from its increasingly static technical proficiency. New blood, not blue blood, preserves old families.

A week or so ago, at a concert in Town Hall, the M.J.Q. made a tentative and unfruitful attempt to solve what may be unsolvable. In three of the numbers, a trumpet (Freddie Hubbard), a tenor saxophone (Jimmy Heath), and a trombone (Curtis Fuller) were added to the group. (The M.J.Q. has taken on occasional single ringers in the past, and with mixed results. Jimmy Giuffre dissolved into the group, while Sonny Rollins, at his most sarcastic, came close to demolishing it. The group's infrequent experiments with the enlarged instrumentation demanded by third-stream music have been more successful.) The outcome was curious. The quartet—Kay in particular—seemed oppressed by the visitors, and the visitors appeared frightened by their hosts. The added horns, none of them first-rate, obscured the delicate ensemble interplay of the group, and were outshone in their solos by Lewis and Jackson. To be sure, it was pleasant to hear such Lewis melodies as "Odds Against Tomorrow," "Django," and "Two Degrees East, Three Degrees West" spelled out loud and clear by horns. But this much was only superficial; part of the appeal of Lewis's work, as we have come to expect, is to hear what the M.J.Q. will do with it. There was a second, if lesser, innovation during the evening. The group played, in addition to its customary selection of Lewis pieces and standards, two originals by outsiders—"Lonely Woman," by Ornette Coleman, and "Why Are You Blue?," by a young West Coast composer-arranger named Gary McFarland. Coleman's melody has an opaque, keening quality, and the M.J.Q., perhaps out of sheer awe, tended to be smothered by it. Or perhaps the group, accustomed to trimming and sharpening its materials over a period of years, has not yet digested it. The group displayed, rather than played, the number. McFarland's tune, an attractive, more accessible affair, was given a sure, relaxed rendition. It was the sort of thing, indeed, that might have been written for the M.J.Q.

The rest of the concert, undiluted and unalloyed, was flawless. There were a very fast "How High the Moon," which has slowly grown into a solo vehicle for Jackson; several of Lewis's *commedia dell'arte* pieces, performed with a lot more gristle than is usual (a couple of them were intricate and outright rhythmic studies, and to hell with the gentle melodies); some ingratiating Lewis ballet music, done with equal push; several blues; "God Rest Ye Merry, Gentlemen"; and a ballad. Lewis coined fresh aphorisms in nearly every number, and Jackson, a passionate and romantic performer whose chosen instrument is just not up to transmitting his vigor and inspiration, was especially orotund. Heath, the M.J.Q.'s All-America center, was exactly that. And Kay got about as much color and dynamics out of his drums as is possible. He shifted constantly between his four exquisitely pitched ride cymbals. (Most young drummers have one or two, and they generally sound alike.) He used finger cymbals, his hands, and the metal loops on his wire brushes in place of sticks. He was never obtrusive, never retiring. In short, he provided the sort of infectious, steadily expanding beat that his model, Sidney Catlett, is still celebrated for.

Masterly Milquetoast

Two of the most elusive and fascinating jazz pianists are Count Basie and Duke Ellington. Though dissimilar stylistically, they have much in common. They are the last of the great graduates of the school of Harlem stride pianists founded by James P. Johnson, furthered by Fats Waller, and presided over now by such elders as Willie the Lion Smith and Luckey Roberts. They are, like most stride pianists, irresistible ensemble pianists, who with their left hands alone can make any band pick up its bed and run. Despite their proved skill as soloists, they are outrageously modest and have steadfastly refused to consider themselves first-rate solo performers. Accordingly, each has recorded just one album of piano solos (with rhythm accompaninent), and once every blue moon has been persuaded to sit in with recording groups, generally with excellent effect. Finally, each is a witty and original stylist. But here the similarities cease. Basie's style is a rhythmic study in rests, occasionally broken by simple right-hand chords or single notes so judiciously placed and sparingly chosen that they suggest impeccably worn jewels. It is stride piano edited, honed, and rubbed into a laconic, semi-comic shape one never tires of. It is Hemingway minus the "truly"s, "and"s, and "good"s. Ellington is twice as adventurous. He has taken the Harlem style apart and rebuilt it, with Gothic flourishes, into an infinitely more imposing structure. He has replaced the ump-chump ump-chump of the left hand with startling off-beat chords and generous basso profundo booms. He has added populous dissonances and far-out chords. And into these he has worked crooked arpeggios—directionless, seemingly drunken ones—and handsome upper-register necklaces of notes that poke harmless fun at James P.'s often lacy right-hand garlands. As such, Ellington's piano style has had a good deal of subtle influence, particularly on Thelonious Monk and Cecil Taylor; it takes iconoclasts to hear one.

It was, then, a pleasant shock when Charles Schwartz, the producer of the superior "Jazz Profiles" series of recitals, announced that Ellington would appear, for the first time in a concert, as a solo pianist, an event that took place in the Museum of Modern Art last Thursday. Needless to say, it is extremely difficult to do well what you are wholeheartedly convinced you cannot do. Ellington regrettably hid for most of the evening—behind his unfailing graciousness, behind his compositions, and behind his accompanists, Aaron Bell and Sam Woodyard, who appeared in the second half of the concert. In the first half, Ellington set forth, in perfect cocktail-piano fashion, six of his more unfamiliar pieces—"New York City Blues," "Blue Belles of Harlem," "The Clothèd Woman," "Reflections in D," a selection from the "Deep South Suite," and "New World A'Comin'." It was a swooning, impressionistic performance that magnified the numbers' virtues and blurred Ellington. After the intermission, Ellington at last gave the impression that he was about to let go. He played several inspiriting choruses of "Take the 'A' Train" (mainly, this part of the program was given over to the works of Billy Strayhorn), and then, changing his mind, gradually handed over the proceedings to Bell and Woodyard, who were allotted a number apiece. (Bell is an accomplished, tonally uncertain Blanton admirer; however, Woodyard, a handsome man who sings a steady song of appreciative grunts and exclamations while he plays, is a caricature of a drummer.) Ellington raced through his customary medley of old pieces, and, again hinting at concealed riches, closed with a delightful "Dancers in Love" that was full of sly, uppity stride-piano figures. After this he retired into his stage presence, disarmingly stating that he was no match for Waller, Tatum, Johnson, etc., and left the stage. Ellington the pianist, having darted nervously out from under his bushel, had vanished once more.

Mechanic

THE MUNIFICENT RELEASE by Columbia of "The Fletcher Henderson Story: A Study in Frustration," which contains sixty-four numbers (on four L.P.s) recorded between 1923 and 1938, is somewhat like reissuing Dr. Johnson's *Dictionary*. Both Henderson's band and Johnson's work were seminal affairs, both were training schools, both were widely copied, both had serious faults, and both, despite their considerable period appeal, are outdated. At the same time, the Henderson album unintentionally reaffirms the theory that the most lasting music of the big-band era, which began around 1925 and ended during the Second World

War, was provided not by the big bands but by countless small swing groups. Though obscured by the bluster of the larger groups, these thrived in the thirties and early forties. A few were permanent or nearly permanent groups, others were drawn from the big bands for informal recording sessions. The full-time small bands were led by Red Norvo, Joe Marsala, Roy Eldridge, Bunny Berigan, Stuff Smith, John Kirby, Adrian Rollini, Frankie Newton, and Fats Waller. The best of the myriad recording groups were organized by Teddy Wilson, Mezz Mezzrow, Red Allen, Lionel Hampton, Sidney Bechet, and various Ellington sidemen, or appeared under names like the Kansas City Six, the Chocolate Dandies, and the Varsity Seven. The small Goodman and Artie Shaw combinations were both in-the-flesh and recording groups. The recordings made by all these bands generally followed these patterns: arranged ensembles–solos–arranged ensembles, or solos–arranged ensembles, or solos–jammed ensembles, or unadorned solos. Some groups were miniature big bands, others were purely improvisatory. Most important, the recordings were relaxed and impromptu; they abound in clams, exhilaration, and sterling solos. (However, the Goodman, Ellington, Kirby, and Basie groups were as finished as anything jazz had produced.) There are two everlasting exceptions to this small-swing-group theory—the big bands of Duke Ellington and Count Basie. Both these bands resembled small groups, though in different ways. Ellington used massed instruments only to set the tone or melody of a piece, and tightly blended his instrumental sections, or parts of them, with his soloists. One was conscious not of size but of continually shifting play of melodies, textures, and colors, in which the soloists and ensembles had a kind of familial relationship. There was no military display, no bunched redcoats potting away at the soloists. The Basie band achieved its lightness and seeming smallness through simple, often poignantly *played* ensemble riffs, which were handed around with a casualness and lack of emphasis that buoyed up the frequent solos. Moreover, the Ellington and Basie bands had unique, easily identifiable styles. Henderson's band, on the other hand, was big, noisy, imitable, and peculiarly flavorless. It was the sort of thick-waisted assemblage that invites weighing and measuring. Indeed, Henderson, along with Don Redman and Benny Carter, who wrote his arrangements before he himself took over, invented the big band, and was more or less responsible for designing the pantheon later inhabited by—among countless others—Goodman, Shaw, Cab Calloway, Glen Gray, the Dorsey brothers, Charlie Barnet, Woody Herman, and Stan Kenton. But Henderson also invented a problem—successfully skirted by Ellington and Basie, and presently under consideration by Charlie Mingus—that neither he nor any of his imitators solved before the big-band era collapsed: how to squeeze ten to fifteen jazz musicians into a *wasteless* and *flexible* jazz unit.

A calm, tall, poised man with a pleasant, bland face, Henderson was born in Cuthbert, Georgia, in 1898, of parents who were teachers, and died in New York in 1952. He attended Atlanta University, where he majored in chemistry, and in 1920 headed for Columbia and post-graduate work. (Many of the Negro bandleaders of the late twenties and early thirties came from similar backgrounds; fortunately for jazz, it wasn't as easy for even educated Negroes to find jobs as bus drivers and the like as it is now.)

Henderson, an easygoing follow-your-nose soul who had been taught piano by his mother, fell into music, and formed his first band in 1923. The rest of his career was equally rudderless. He was a fair-to-poor businessman, a spotty disciplinarian (his often great and ingeniously chosen sidemen eventually became a collection of prima donnas who were frequently tardy, heavy-drinking, and quarrelsome), and the kind of man who regards opportunities as insults. Toward the end of the twenties, Henderson suffered severe injuries in an automobile accident, which apparently converted him from a relaxed man into a lazy one. As a result, he never quite reached the top, and after a fitful decade and a half as a bandleader, he went into semi-retirement. However, Henderson did succeed, in an ironic fashion. In 1935, he began writing arrangements for Goodman. It was an indenture that lasted well over a decade and that had much to do with Goodman's fame. For Goodman's band was largely a popularization of Henderson's, down to the very solos. It is hard, in fact, not to think of Goodman's band as the Benny Goodman-Fletcher Henderson Orchestra.

Henderson was more of a talented accidentalist than an originator. His first band had, like the large white dance bands that had preceded it, nine or ten men and an instrumentation of two trumpets, one trombone, two or three reeds, piano, banjo, tuba, and drums. It employed brief solos and arrangements that alternately sighed and bumped along on fashionable clarinet trios and two-beat now-you-hear-us, now-you-don't rhythm sections. Then, in 1924, Louis Armstrong joined the band and Don Redman began to take hold. Redman's arrangements sidestepped New Orleans polyphony and served up smooth, melodic variations written for specific sections of the band and often set in call-and-response patterns. And Armstrong's imaginativeness completed the shift from an imitation white dance orchestra to a jazz band. Between 1925, when Armstrong departed, and 1930, the band began collecting superior soloists like Joe Smith, Rex Stewart, Benny Morton, Jimmy Harrison, Tommy Ladnier, and Bobby Stark. It also collected Benny Carter, as an arranger, alto saxophonist, and clarinetist. Carter's arrangements were in many ways the most accomplished ones Henderson ever used. Carter wrote limber, seemingly improvised passages for the reeds and light, complementary brass figures, all of which were immeasurably helped by a steady four-four beat and the substitution of the guitar and string bass for the banjo and tuba. Henderson's own arrangements, which began coming off the presses in quantity after Carter left, were far more formal. The sections shouted stubbornly at one another or were mixed lumpishly in colorless voicings. They called for more instruments, and those instruments called for even more instruments. But Henderson's arrangements, along with those of his younger brother Horace, achieved considerable polish (though also predictability) and served as the latticework for the magnificent soloists who continued to file in and out of the band—Claude Jones, Cootie Williams, Red Allen, J. C. Higginbotham, Dickie Wells, and (in the last years) Roy Eldridge, Chu Berry, Sid Catlett, Emmett Berry, and Ben Webster. Stark stayed on until 1933 and Coleman Hawkins until 1934, and Walter Johnson, who—Chick Webb excepted —was the first of the big-band drummers, was with Henderson almost continually from 1928 until the end. The band reached two peaks—between 1932 and 1934, and briefly in 1936.

But even in these years something was missing. The foursquare arrangements, though adept, were dull and gray, and were often executed accordingly. Unlike those used by Ellington and Basie, they seemed unrelated to the soloists; they filled the ears and they filled space. The puzzle of what to do with the twelve and more instruments slowly accumulated through the years was met simply by pressing them into four regiments, which exchanged riffs and fragmentary melodic variations or marched stoutly together, parting here and there to let a soloist through. (This failure had a good deal to do with the revolution eventually known as bebop.) Yet the soloists *were* the Henderson band, and it is Red Allen, Eldridge, Hawkins, Benny Morton, Claude Jones, Benny Carter, Rex Stewart, Joe Smith, J. C. Higginbotham, and Bobby Stark who provide the excitement in Henderson's recordings. To be sure, it has frequently been pointed out that Henderson's band almost never came through properly on records. And barring the solos, many of the numbers in the Columbia album do have a stale, time-clock air. Some are even pallid. But there are exceptions—a very fast "Chinatown" (1930); Carter's arrangement of "Sweet and Hot" (1931); Horace Henderson's "Hot and Anxious" (1931), in which some of the riffs that became "In the Mood," "Swingin' the Blues," and "One O'Clock Jump" are three-dimensionally on view (Henderson *was* a star-crossed man); Horace Henderson's "Comin' and Goin'" (1931), with exemplary Stark and Morton solos; the various "King Porter Stomp"'s (1932, 1933), which are—some of the

Mechanic   205

solos included—the Goodman band to come, and which reveal Hawkins entering his great middle period; Horace Henderson's arrangement of Hawkins's "Queer Notions" (1933), a fascinating, semiatonal avant-garde piece, with solos to match by the composer and Red Allen; and the celebrated 1936 "Christopher Columbus," "Stealin' Apples," and "Blue Lou," all of them brilliantly dominated by Roy Eldridge and Chu Berry.

Most of the drawbacks in the Columbia set are unavoidable. The sound of the pre-1930 records is generally sandy and remote, though it is better than on the original 78s, and there is a complete blank between 1933 and 1936, and for a good reason: five celebrated sides, made under Horace Henderson's name for English Parlophone in 1933, were unavailable for the album, as were the sixteen or so superior numbers set down the following year for Decca and Victor. (Only one of these is now available.) Accordingly, the accent in the album falls rather heavily on the early academically-interesting-only years. (However, none of the first-rate small-band efforts made in 1930 by the Chocolate Dandies, who were drawn from the band, are included. And perhaps wisely so; they would have blotted out everything around them.) The set is rounded off with a sizable booklet, which has good photographs and an excellent account of Henderson's career by Frank Driggs. There is also a brief memoir by John Hammond, who, as Henderson's friend and as the head of Columbia's current reissue program, deserves high commendation for restoring the master machine that produced the machines that eventually ate it.

Slow Sleeper

UNTIL the late twenties, the trombone, that difficult and beautiful instrument, was the clown of jazz. In the ensembles it was used to plug holes, provide comic smears and asides (Kid Ory's "Muskrat Ramble" celebrated these functions), and anchor the trumpet and clarinet. It was an infrequent and unsteady solo instrument, and was limited to whisky-baritone paraphrasings of the melody. Then the big bands, two or three trombones strong, came along, and by 1930 first-rate trombonists who could both read and improvise were everywhere. Among them were Miff Mole (largely a small-band performer), J. C. Higginbotham, Dickie Wells, Benny Morton, Jimmy Harrison, Claude Jones, Sandy Williams, and Jack Teagarden. Harrison, who died in 1931, is generally thought of as the first swing trombonist. To be sure, he helped shape Williams, Morton, and possibly Jones, but Higginbotham and Wells were already on their respective trapezes (if Higginbotham listened to anybody, it was to Mole), and when a fully formed Teagarden arrived in New York, in 1927, he astonished everyone, including Harrison. Unfortunately, the trombone has never again equalled this collective burst of glory. (Brad Gowans was a notable maverick, who ended up, for better or worse, in the Dixieland school, while the pretty and/or corny trombonists, who had little to do with jazz, included Tommy Dorsey, Bobby Byrne, Russ Morgan, Will Bradley, and Jack Jenney.) The big bands began to disappear in the mid-forties, and Bill Harris and Trummy Young became the unstable bridge between the older men and bebop, which produced J. J. Johnson and Kai Winding, fine technicians who figure-skate rather than improvise. Among the younger men, who are faced with the mists of abstract jazz, only Willie Dennis, an apoplectic performer, and Jimmy Knepper, who has learned from Johnson and the likes of Higginbotham, are attempting to expand the possibilities of their instrument. (Bob Brookmeyer, like Ruby Braff and Gerry Mulligan, is an accomplished neo-swing musician.) As a result, when one wants to hear a *trombone*, one turns to Vic Dickenson, who emerged in the late thirties, or to Ellington's Lawrence Brown, to Morton, and particularly to Teagarden, who is fifty-six, and who reached perfection before the present generation was born. (Wells and Higginbotham are waning. Williams has retired, and Mole and Jones are dead.)

An inscrutable combination of temperament, accident, skill, and faddism has made certain great jazz musicians both famous and wealthy. Others, like Teagarden, are merely famous. Teagarden's career, in fact, has been a marathon scramble. From 1921 until his arrival in New York, he jobbed around the Southwest with such men as Peck Kelley and Willard Robison, and then existed largely on recording dates before he joined Ben Pollack, in 1928. He left Pollack in 1933, starved briefly, and was hired by Paul Whiteman, who housed him for four or five years. Teagarden then formed his own big band, a talented and unsuccessful group that moved back and forth across the country until its leader, weary of nursemaiding fifteen-odd people around, gave it up, in 1947, and joined Louis Armstrong's All Stars. He stayed for four years with this disheveled, bejeweled group, which also included Barney Bigard, Earl Hines, and Sidney Catlett. Since then, he has led an increasingly adept small band of his own. Teagarden is often lumped with Eddie Condon and the Chicago boys, but he is really a lone wolf who has worked with dance bands and swing bands of all sizes as well as with neo-New Orleans and Dixieland groups. His style, equally unclannish, apparently popped whole out of the Southwestern soil. (He was born in Vernon, Texas.) For Teagarden has said that his influences, if any, were Bessie Smith, Negro church singers, and Indian music he heard as a boy in Nebraska.

Teagarden's appearance is as singular as his playing and singing. A tall, handsomely constructed man, he has a square, rocky, Indian face (he is of Germanic descent), topped by black, closely combed hair, and a casual, smiling demeanor. (Once, asked why he slept so much, he replied that, like most Southerners, he was a slow sleeper.) His trombone style is chiefly marked by a nasal, bright-gray tone and an apparent insouciance which conceals an iron restraint. It is a unique style, which has not changed, except for steady but microscopic refinements, for nearly three decades. Indeed, it is impossible to think of a poor Teagarden vocal or solo. (Because of the demands of their instrument, trombonists are probably the most erratic jazz instrumentalists.) Teagarden has developed a sustaining set of mannerisms—lazy glissandos, abrupt, change-of-pace triplets and runs, and an occasional hoarseness of tone—that offer a seemingly bland and mechanical façade. But Teagarden demands close listening, for he uses these devices in oblique, shifting combinations that invariably catch one off balance. In short, he seems to have in mind a sort of Platonic master solo, from which he adapts the solo he actually plays—a subtly accented variation. His slow blues are extraordinary. He will open in the low register, hold the note just long enough to snare the listener, slide quietly into the middle register (while blending in a few up-and-down configurations), then, increasing his volume slightly, move even higher, and fall away into a hoarse, careless blue note. Then he may shift into a rapid, soft-shoe series of triplets, pause for the first time, and shape a declamatory phrase, reach swiftly upward again, and drop softly back to his starting point. It is a poured rather than a played solo, done so offhandedly that one doesn't realize its technical wizardry until a second or third hearing. His ballad numbers receive the same gentle reshufflings and windings, and so do his up-tempo statements, which come closest to letting the constant emotion inside his work into the open. His reluctance to rant and weep in public has made Teagarden one of the few genuinely cool jazz musicians. Trombonists have always been prone to bosomy vibratos, upper-register peeps, and tuba blasts. But Teagarden will have none of these. When he leaves the middle range, uses a vibrato, alters his volume, or fashions a coda, he does these things in a gloved way. The results are painless, graceful, and never slick.

Teagarden's superlative singing is a direct extension of this coolness. Although his baritone voice, which has deepened considerably in the past ten years, is strikingly close to his trombone, it is smoother and almost completely legato in style. Indeed, Teagarden's slurred, rubbing delivery of lyrics suggests that he is trying to abolish consonants in favor of a new, vowels-only language. At the same time, his singing has both the unobtrusive amiability of a Bing Crosby and a behind-the-beat jazz intensity that no other jazz singer has possessed. He neither moans nor shouts; instead, he undersings, flattering the ear and forcing one to listen.

Teagarden's recent recordings have done him little justice. He has been laced into tight Dixieland bands and plastered down with strings. He has used exhausted materials and appeared with exhausted musicians. Some of these things are true of his newest efforts—"Chicago and All That Jazz!" (done just before the television show of the same name) and "Mis'ry and the Blues: Jack Teagarden and His Sextet" (Verve). Teagarden is weighted down in the first recording with Joe Sullivan, Eddie Condon, Jimmy McPartland, Bud Freeman, and Gene Krupa. But he rises easily out of the swamps. On the first half of the record (he is heard only briefly on the second side), he plays marvelously in a slow blues, "Logan Square," and sings three classic choruses in it; solos well in "Chicago"; sings another classic chorus in "After You've Gone"; and begins a magnificent chorus of "China Boy," then is abruptly replaced by another soloist. The rest of the record is a shambles. Pee Wee Russell, who recently escaped from his Dixieland bondage, sounds exactly like a recaptured slave. McPartland quavers. Freeman baubles. And Sullivan, Bob Haggart, and Krupa resemble nervous cattle.

The second record, done with Teagarden's own group, is a far sweeter affair. Aside from King Oliver's "Froggie Moore Blues," the "Dixieland One-Step," and the "Basin Street Blues," which Teagarden sings and plays as if he had just discovered it (he and Glenn Miller wrote the lyrics in 1929, and Teagarden has probably sung them five days a week ever since), the record consists of a couple of surprisingly charming Willard Robison tunes, "Don't Tell a Man About His Woman" and "Peaceful Valley," and out-of-the-way numbers by Seger Ellis and Charlie La Vere. Teagarden sings in six of the ten numbers and solos in all but one. He is effortless, inspired, and technically perfect. His restrained and helpful accompanists include Don Goldie (a Charlie Shavers admirer whose father played trumpet with Teagarden in Whiteman's band), Don Ewell, and Barrett Deems.

Bless Teagarden, and may he prosper, too.

Third-Stream Music

THAT admirable nonagon, the Renaissance man, is by no means extinct. This intelligence was confirmed recently when I talked with Gunther Schuller, a thirty-six-year-old Castiglione, who is, among other things, composer and chief prophet of "Third-stream" music (six compositions); composer of atonal classical works (over thirty of them, including orchestral, chamber, and vocal compositions); French-horn player (two years with the Cincinnati Symphony, fourteen with the Metropolitan Opera, eventually as its first horn); teacher (horn and composition, for both classical and jazz students); editor (M.J.Q. Music, Inc., a music-publishing firm); music critic (jazz, classical music); lecturer; conductor; author (*Horn Technique,* a book on the art of playing the French horn, and an untitled, unfinished analytical history of jazz); and music commentator on radio (a weekly program on WBAI-FM). When I arrived at Schuller's apartment, on West

Ninetieth Street, I was greeted by my host, who is tall and slightly stooped, and resembles a kindly, unself-conscious John Barrymore. He said that he was finishing a session with a student, and showed me into the living room, which was filled with music manuscripts, records, rolls of tape, books, heaps of papers, music stands, musical instruments, and a couple of barn-door-size loudspeakers. When the student, a pretty Negro girl horn player, had left, Schuller, who looked somewhat haggard and was dressed in a bright checked shirt, olive-drab corduroy trousers, and moccasins (no socks), sat down and leaned intently forward, and I asked him how he managed his nonagonal existence.

"Oh, it's hell in terms of my private life," he said, and laughed. "I used to teach twenty-five hours a week, and now I've cut down to ten. I have just four horn students left, but jazz musicians come to me a good deal for advanced training and I seldom have the guts to turn them down. There aren't many teachers who know both jazz and advanced techniques of classical music. I've just come back from a three-week trip to Europe, and, God, it was marvelous! Seven countries! A new piece of mine, 'Contrasts,' was given its world première at the Donaueschingen Festival, in West Germany. The whole German music scene is outrageously chauvinistic and outrageously avant-garde, and I guess I'm the first American ever commissioned by Donaueschingen. I also lined up outlets for M.J.Q. Music and hunted all over for European jazz musicians for the International Jazz Festival, which is being sponsored by the President's Music Committee in Washington in the spring. I didn't get into Poland, where a big festival was going on, and where Friedrich Gulda was appearing as a jazz baritone saxophonist. But I found a superb Yugo-slavian trumpeter in the Dixieland tradition and a good Miles Davis-type Swedish trumpeter." Schuller leaned back and laughed again.

"What about the third stream?" I asked.

"I coined the term as an *adjective*, not a noun," he replied, hunching forward excitedly. "I never thought it would become a slogan, a catchword. I hit upon the term simply as a handle, and it has achieved a kind of pompousness and finality that are totally inaccurate. This music is only *beginning*. I conceive of it as the result of two tributaries— one from the stream of classical music and one from the other stream, jazz—that have recently flowed out toward each other in the space between the two main streams. The two main streams are left undisturbed, or mostly so. I'm often criticized for trying to *force* classical music and jazz together. But this is nonsense. There will always be jazz musicians who have absolutely no knowledge of classical music, and classical musicians and composers who abhor jazz. But if a person has been exposed to both streams honestly and thoroughly, it's bound to show up in his creative products, and those of us who see this possible alignment have the great privilege of working toward it. I conceive that sooner or later the musical public will have more awareness of this situation. I see it beginning everywhere. Kids in universities where I speak think nothing of playing a Charlie Parker record right after *Eine Kleine Nachtmusik*. Third-stream music is a stylistic question more than anything else. The main differences between jazz and non-jazz are the improvisation and the naturally based and intuitive inflections of jazz. The new music is, in part, a process of joining jazz inflections and phrasing to the more set phrases

Dinosaurs in the Morning   214

and techniques of non-jazz. The point is, though, to have the two approaches occur *simultaneously*. Up to now, they have usually been linked *alternately*. There are many other problems. The improviser has to fit himself to the composer, and the composer to the improviser. When Ornette Coleman performed my 'Abstraction,' he already knew my non-jazz music, and I had listened closely to him. He had given me a wonderful sense of freedom, because his horizons are so wide. I hope that classical music will get from jazz a spontaneity and naturalness of phrasing that it no longer has. Of course, contemporary classical music *is* becoming more improvisational. It's different from the kind of improvisation you get in jazz, though—less melodic, and more concentrated on ensemble textures and the like. But then ninety-eight per cent of of the classical musicians simply don't have the sense of timing that jazz musicians have. All those ragged ensembles and sloppy notes! When I write a run of eighth notes for a violin section, I generally get back in performance about a tenth of what I've written. Centuries of abuse have brought this about. I'm convinced that in baroque music the performers had good timing. They had to have it."

I asked Schuller, whose eloquence had left him momentarily limp, to tell me how his career had got started.

"My father has been a violinist with the New York Philharmonic for thirty-eight years," he said, working up a new head of steam. "I heard music from the day I was born. I absorbed a fantastic amount of music. I remember sitting in the bathtub with my brother when I was only six and the two of us singing the whole *Tannhäuser* Overture together and imitating all the instruments. I started school in Germany, and when I came back, at eleven, I had a good boy soprano's voice, and was sent to the St. Thomas Church Choir School. They discovered there that I could sight-read like a whiz. When I started studying music, it was a process not of learning the cold and new but of recognizing things that I had known subconsciously all along. My first instrument was the flute, which I took up in my early teens. My father, who never pushed me, said whatever you do, don't play the violin. Violinists were starving to death in New York then. One of his friends in the orchestra suggested he try me on the French horn. Wind players—particularly American ones—were still terribly scarce. So I studied horn for two years, and at sixteen I quit school and got a job with the Ballet Theatre Orchestra, at a hundred and twenty-five dollars a week. I never went back to school, and have no diploma of any kind. I joined the Cincinnati Symphony the next year, and made my début as a soloist and a composer with my Concerto for Horn and Orchestra. I was nineteen. I was hired by the Met in 1945 and left in 1959. I got interested in jazz in Cincinnati, when I first heard Duke Ellington. It was a stunning experience. I made entire scores of Ellington recordings —things that had never been completely annotated before. If I could work full time on my book on jazz, I'd finish it in three or four months; as it is, I turn down quite a few commissions for composing. We know all about *who* made jazz but not *how* and *why*. My first chapter is an investigation of what happened here in the nineteenth century, and I hope it will blast things wide open. I studied A. M. Jones's extraordinary two-volume work on African music, and I've used his findings—he's made complete scores of pieces that go on for hours —in examining, say, the slave songs first published in America in 1863. The results are quite astonishing. African music is the most complex and sophisticated music in the world, and jazz is—or was, in its primitive stages—a simplification of its polyrhythmic structure. Jazz is now heading back toward this complexity. I've gone through the Folkways Records catalogue and found things like three girls down South singing a strange little song that is practically identical with one recorded about ten years ago in equatorial Africa. I'm on the track of the origin of the blues, which may have started in India and traveled through the Arab countries, and then to Spain and/or to Africa and on to the Caribbean and New Orleans. I've got masses of material all ready to put on the page, but the time—where is the time?"

Index

Index

Index 224